Nappy Free Baby

A practical guide to baby-led potty training from birth

Amber Hatch

Vermilion
LONDON

1 3 5 7 9 10 8 6 4 2

Vermilion, an imprint of Ebury Publishing,
20 Vauxhall Bridge Road,
London SW1V 2SA

Vermilion is part of the Penguin Random House group of companies
whose addresses can be found at global.penguinrandomhouse.com

Copyright © Amber Hatch 2015
Illustrations copyright © Alex Ogg 2015

Amber Hatch has asserted her right to be identified as the author of this Work
in accordance with the Copyright, Designs and Patents Act 1988

First published by Vermilion in 2015

www.eburypublishing.co.uk

A CIP catalogue record for this book is available from the British Library

ISBN 9780091955335

Printed and bound in Great Britain by Clays Ltd, St Ives PLC

Penguin Random House is committed to a sustainable future for our business, our readers
and our planet. This book is made from Forest Stewardship Council® certified paper.

MIX
Paper from
responsible sources
FSC® C018179

*For all the babies and their families
who shared their experiences of BLPT with me.*

Contents

Introduction

I'll never forget the first time I held my newborn baby over a potty. In fact, it was an ice-cream tub. It was 2008 and my baby was five weeks old. It was about seven in the morning. Like all new mums, I was tired; my baby, of course, had woken me up for milk a few times in the night. But the thing that had been really bothering me was the grunting and squirming that she had been doing on and off for the last couple of hours. It had happened for a few days now. Something was preventing her from settling into a deep sleep, and I was too keyed into her movements to ignore it and get back to sleep myself. I kept trying to feed her yet she wouldn't latch on.

Then I remembered a technique I'd read about on the web a few days before – 'elimination communication' they had called it. So I found the ice-cream tub, and duly stripped off my baby's nappy. I balanced her wobbly back against my tummy while I sat on the bed, and I supported her by her thighs over the tub.

I didn't have to wait long. Within a few seconds the tension in her little body peaked and almost immediately a wee trickled into the tub. Wow. Somehow I hadn't been expecting it, even though that's why I was holding her. And then there was more – one big grunt and this time a bright orange poo squirted out into the tub, and I could feel all the tension in her body slip away. After I had scrabbled around for something to wipe her with – careful not to knock over the tub – I put her nappy back on and we snuggled down for a feed. This time, she latched on without a fuss and gently dropped off into a calm sleep. But by now, I was too excited to sleep.

Why had no one mentioned this before? Here was a technique that could help my baby feel more comfortable, and that could help me get more sleep. And it was so easy. And so fun! Surely every mum should learn this in antenatal classes? From that moment on, I was inspired to keep holding my baby out over the potty. The more I did it, and the more I learnt about the process, the more excited I got. Here was a method of baby care that was easy and practical, and I kept discovering more and more benefits.

I told everyone I knew: mums, dads, even people without children, even people I didn't know. Some people got as excited about it as me; some thought I was a little crazy. But I didn't stop there. Within a few weeks I had set up a free monthly support group for parents wanting to give it a go in Oxford. But I still felt that more people needed access to information about this simple method. It was the world's best-kept secret, yet every parent had a right to know about it. At the time the only information on the web was from American websites. So I set up www.nappyfreebaby.co.uk to provide information to UK parents.

When my son was born in 2011, I had no hesitation about holding him over the potty within hours of his birth. Catching that sticky meconium (the first poo) in a potty was very satisfying. Now, having seen two children through from start to finish, and drawing from the experience of all the families I've worked with, I have a much broader perspective, and a wealth of knowledge. But still I've never lost the sense of excitement that came with that first 'catch'.

I have seen this method used by mums in full-time work, by dads and grandparents. I've seen it practised just every now and then or even as a fully fledged, full-time alternative to nappies. I now know how flexible it can be. You don't have to be any specific type of parent. Nor do you have to sign up to anything. You can try it once and forget about it; and if you've tried it out, it will be an informed decision.

About this book

In this book I will explain how you can introduce your baby to the potty and help keep him cleaner, drier and more comfortable. I call this method 'baby-led potty training' (BLPT for short), although we don't focus on the end result – not for some time, anyway! In the meantime it's a gentle and intuitive way of managing a baby's waste.

The method can help you use fewer nappies, increase your parent–child communication and bypass some of the common pitfalls of delaying toilet training. You can also be 'nappy free'. This term can cause alarm. However, when I say 'nappy free' I really mean this in a broader sense – free from 100 per cent reliance on nappies. Because baby-led potty training enables you to manage your baby's waste in a clean and hygienic way, it *is* possible to bring your baby up completely nappy free if you wish. However, it's also fine (and more common) to use nappies more pragmatically, with nappy-off times at certain periods. Or you can still use the techniques with your baby wearing a nappy between potty trips. All of these variations are fine, and will be explored in detail.

I'll explain exactly what BLPT is and how it works in Chapter 1, along with the main benefits, and I'll explain how practices have changed over time, and why. You can learn how the bladder and bowel function and develop in Chapter 2, plus what skills may be acquired at each stage. Chapter 3 discusses the pros and cons of different starting ages, and Chapters 4–14 provide a complete practical guide to getting started, keeping going and avoiding mistakes. I've dedicated Chapter 8 to special cases, which covers practising BLPT with multiples and if your child has special needs. If you are going back to work, Chapter 12 shows you how to incorporate BLPT into your childcare arrangements.

I also want this book to serve as a guide for those of you wishing to practise baby-led potty training right through to toilet independence. All too often, existing resources on the method fall short of this transition, leaving parents unsure of how to 'finish the process'.

Chapters 15 and 16 address this, showing you how you can help your child move from assisted potty trips to toilet independence, both day and night.

Dotted around the book you'll find the stories and tips of many other parents who have practised BLPT. I found these anecdotes very supportive, useful and often inspiring. I hope you do too.

I've tried to keep the language as self-explanatory as possible, but in case you want to check any definitions you'll find a glossary of the key terms at the back of the book. There's also a resources section with suggestions for further reading, and websites with more information, including up-to-date lists of stockists of specialist BLPT equipment.

Please note that I've used 'he' for babies throughout the book rather than 'he or she', just for ease of reading and consistency. I opted for 'he' over 'she' as some parents think of boys as more difficult to potty train than girls; I didn't want to add fuel to this myth. Both boys and girls are equally receptive to this method.

How to use this book

I've written this book primarily for parents, though I hope that anyone who works with or looks after babies will find it useful too. Below are some specific suggestions for how you might want to use the book, depending on the age of your baby or babies.

If your baby is 0–6 months

You will get the most out of the method (and this book) if your baby is younger than six months. In fact the younger you start, the better. If your baby is under six months, the best way to use this book is to read the first nine chapters straight through. If you are very busy (and what parent isn't?) you may be tempted to skip ahead to Chapter 4, 'Getting Started'. That's fine, but I highly recommend you go back and read the earlier chapters as soon as you can. Knowing the theory behind the method will help you work with and understand your baby. After

Chapter 9, you may want to put this book aside for a few weeks or months, until you are ready to read about the next stages of development.

Alternatively, you may prefer to read right to the end so that you have an overview of how the process will work from start to finish. That's up to you.

You can skip Chapters 11 and 14, as they focus on getting started with an older baby.

If your baby is 6–12 months

If your baby is between 6 and 12 months, you can still reap the benefits of the method. You'll need to read through the earlier chapters to understand how BLPT works. Although Chapter 4, 'Getting Started', is aimed primarily at nought to six months, much of the practicalities apply to an older baby too. I also provide specific details on starting between 6 and 12 months in Chapter 11.

If your baby or toddler is 12–18 months

Babies and toddlers who are older than 12 months can also make use of BLPT. As all families are unique, and babies acquire skills at varying ages, different families will find different sections of the book more relevant. If your child is older than 12 months, it's still really important that you understand the theory behind the method, as explained in the first three chapters, but it's likely that many of the techniques laid out in Chapter 4, 'Getting Started', will no longer apply. Chapters 5 to 9, however, are relevant throughout the 0–18-month period. Chapters 10 and 11, which focus on babies aged 6 to 12 months, may still be useful as there is often overlap between these age ranges. Chapters 13 and 14 should be especially useful as they focus on the 12–18-month period.

Over 18 months

If your toddler is over 18 months, and has already been using a potty for some time, then Chapters 13, 15 and 16 will be particularly useful to you in helping your child make the transition to toilet independence. With the possible exception of the 'Getting Started' chapters (4, 11 and 14), the rest of the book also contains interesting and relevant information that will help you better understand your child.

Whatever stage your baby is at, I hope this book will empower you with the knowledge and the tools you need to try out BLPT for yourself. I want you to have a *real* choice about how you keep your baby clean. Enjoy your journey of discovery!

Chapter 1

What is Baby-Led Potty Training?

At the heart of the baby-led potty-training method is the technique of *pottying*: when parents actively encourage their baby to pass waste. A baby is helped into an optimal posture, in an appropriate place for urination or defecation, normally *outside* of his nappy. This can be done occasionally to settle a windy newborn or as a complete alternative to nappies, and anywhere in between. I'll refer to this act throughout the book as both 'holding your baby out' and 'offering the potty'; I use these terms interchangeably – you can decide which position, and what receptacle, is most appropriate at any given time.

How it works in a nutshell

You need to hold your baby over (or sit him on) a potty or other receptacle. Letting air get to the bottom area by removing the nappy triggers a reflex which helps your baby to pass wind, urine or a bowel movement. The position also encourages the release of the sphincters and pelvic floor. Your baby then defecates and urinates in the potty rather than in his nappy. You can learn to recognise when your baby needs to pass waste, and your baby learns to release his bladder and bowels at the right time, through association.

'I really like that Sam very obviously "gets it". It isn't just timing, as some people have suggested. If I hold him and he doesn't need to go, he still grunts and shows that he is trying and knows what it is all about. Also we seem to be able to do it part-time – as in the modern world with car journeys and other people not practising the same method, we need flexibility to use nappies sometimes.'

Leila, mum to Sam, five months

Full-time, part-time or occasionally?

On one end of the spectrum, you can use this system as a full-time alternative to conventional nappies (although most families use some kind of nappy system as a backup, particularly in the first year). However, most parents use BLPT on a more casual basis, in conjunction with nappies. For example, your baby can wear nappies and you can offer the potty at change times or if he seems particularly uncomfortable. In fact, many families don't think of it as potty training at all. You can also just use the method occasionally, for example when your baby seems to be having difficulty passing a bowel movement or when he has nappy rash, or in the first few weeks when your baby is unsettled.

Some families start with BLPT at birth and continue until their child is toilet independent, while others only use it every now and again. There will be different pay-offs roughly according to the effort you put in. So that you can see how BLPT might fit into your family, I've gathered a few examples of the many different ways you can use this method:

A full-time alternative

Caroline started BLPT when her daughter Zara was around two months. She found it really easy to recognise when Zara needed to wee or poo, so tried to get her nappy off whenever she thought she needed to pass waste – she would aim to 'catch' pretty much everything. Between potty trips, Zara generally wore nappies 'just in case' but for the vast majority of the time the nappy she was wearing was clean and dry. She normally had one or two wet nappies – or 'misses' – a day, which Caroline tried to change immediately. She rarely soiled her nappy. At around 10 months, Caroline found it easier for Zara to wear training pants or tracksuit bottoms. Occasional poo misses disappeared around 14 months. Although she still had the odd wee accident, Zara was generally dry from 20 months.

Intelligent nappy-free time

Becky didn't set out to practise baby-led potty training, but she did want to offer her baby plenty of nappy-free time. Often, when she was at home, she would remove her son's nappy so that he could roll around without it on his play mat. It made sense to her to offer him the potty beforehand. While he had his nappy off, she would offer the potty every half hour or so. He quickly learnt to use the potty and he would rarely wee (and never poo) on the mat. This made nappy-free time much more manageable, and encouraged her to do it for longer. She didn't offer the potty at any other time. As he got older, there were stretches when she was busy and didn't offer the potty at all. The practice naturally evolved into potty training, as she began to leave him without a nappy for longer and longer. At 18 months, he would reliably take himself to the potty at home when he was naked. She took him out of nappies for good just before he was two.

A routine-based approach

Lillian held her baby out/offered a potty every time she changed her baby, so around five times a day. She would often catch a wee at those times, and she probably caught about half of his poos too. Sometimes there would be nothing in the potty, and the rest of the time he was happy to use the nappy. Lillian was using cloth nappies and she found that this system made using them significantly easier, reducing the number of dirty nappies used. She continued this approach into his toddlerhood, and it became a gentle transition to toilet independence.

Focus on bowel movements

Jane used nappies normally, except she offered the potty whenever she noticed her baby straining to pass a bowel movement, which was once or twice a day. In this way she went for many weeks at a time without having to change a dirty nappy. Once her baby reached toddlerhood she was less interested in using the potty, and Jane offered it less and less. She potty trained easily at a conventional age.

Helping constipation

Kristina first came across BLPT, when her baby was four months old. Her baby had not passed a bowel movement for six days. Although her health visitor had said it wasn't a problem for breastfed babies, she was concerned because she knew her baby was uncomfortable. She had heard about BLPT so went along to a workshop at a children's centre where they were explaining the method. At the workshop, she undid her baby's nappy and held her on the potty for the first time. Within a minute her baby's face went bright red and everyone heard the sound of a very large poo exploding into the potty. Kristina was much relieved – and presumably her baby was too. Kristina continued to use the technique every now and again, whenever she suspected that her baby was having trouble passing a bowel movement.

Soothing windy babies

Mark and Kate's baby girl started to suffer from colic when she was around three weeks old. During her crying spells, her parents would try anything to soothe her. Mark heard about BLPT from a colleague when his baby was five weeks old. Although nothing seemed to settle her for long when she was in her worst periods, Mark found that holding her in an optimal position for passing waste did help his daughter to expel gas and poo. This soothed her for a while – sometimes enough to enable her to fall asleep – and it significantly reduced the amount of time she was spending crying.

So you can see that BLPT can be used in many ways, to a greater or lesser extent. There is no one 'right' way to do BLPT. Some parents just use the technique when their babies are very little to help settle them. They may stop after a few weeks and then use nappies until typically they decide to potty train at a conventional age. Some parents start when their babies are sitting up. Some just aim to catch bowel movements. Every family will approach the method differently, and all of these variations are completely fine; the aim of this book is to give you the tools and the confidence you need to try it for yourself. Once you have honed the skill, you'll get a feel for how much, and how often, is right for you.

Benefits

There are four distinct outcomes of practising BLPT:

1. Less waste in your baby's nappies
2. An increase in positive parent–child communication
3. More comfort for your baby
4. Your baby becomes accustomed to using the potty

These four outcomes lead to a diverse range of benefits, the most important of which I'll cover now. Most of these can be experienced regardless of whether you hold your baby out just once a fortnight, or many times a day. You'll start seeing gains straight away, and you'll no doubt discover your own unique benefits too.

1. Less waste in your baby's nappies

Perhaps the most obvious outcome of BLPT is that more of your baby's waste will go straight down the drain. This means many benefits, including that your baby will use fewer nappies, and will spend less time sitting in soiled and wet ones:

Fewer dirty nappies

Because BLPT can be very successful with bowel movements, many parents find that they rarely need to change a dirty nappy. Some parents just concentrate on catching poos in their baby's first year. This is particularly beneficial to parents using cloth nappies; without poos there's no scraping or sluicing the dirty nappy in the loo, no stinky nappy buckets, no need for nappy liners. It's pretty good for disposable users too; I'm sure most parents prefer to avoid changing a dirty nappy if there is the option! And it certainly helps cut the financial cost of disposables.

> 'I started BLPT when Max was 3 months, and he was done by 21 months. I caught virtually every poo in that time, so I must have saved over 500 dirty nappy changes. That's about £100 saved in disposables, straight off – more if you count the wet ones – plus the fact he was probably out of nappies earlier.'
>
> **Adriana, mum to Max, three years**

Less nappy rash

Exposure to urine and faeces, perfumes, detergents and wipes may all cause nappy rash. Experts agree that nappy-free time can prevent nappy rash. BLPT is a practical way for you to do that: there will be much less mess if you offer the potty beforehand. You may start to offer spontaneous nappy-free time immediately after your baby has used the potty too.

Some parents find nappy-free time impractical and they prefer to keep their babies in a nappy most or all of the time. BLPT can help avoid nappy rash in these circumstances too. Every time you help your baby wee or poo outside his nappy – whether that's a few hours once a week or just at convenient times – you are helping his nappy stay cleaner and drier for longer, which all helps to prevent nappy rash.

> 'I started BLPT out of desperation as my daughter was pooing so frequently she had developed really bad nappy rash. As this is now settled we use nappies most of the time but offer the toilet/potty during nappy changes and after sleeps. I hope to get the nappies off more after the winter when we have some warmer weather.'
>
> **Rachel, mum to Meagan, six months**

A cleaner process

BLPT can also make for a much cleaner and easier process too, as these parents found:

'I used to have nappy explosions all the time. Once, when Arthur was a month old, I had to change his clothes four times during a trip to a café. After I started doing BLPT I never had any again.'

Sarah, mum to Arthur, 15 months

'It's always a shock to me when he poos in his nappy. Luckily it's pretty rare! The clean-up process is so much quicker and easier when it goes straight in the potty. It's more hygienic too.'

Danielle, mum to Jack, five months

'Because my son (who is four months) can wee anywhere, I don't worry about finding a change table for him. He so rarely poos in his nappy, and if it's a wee I can just change him on my knee or even standing up. I use so few wipes and nappies that I don't bother carrying a change bag around any more. I feel really liberated! I can't remember the last time I had to carry a pooey nappy around in my handbag.'

Lisa, mum to Tom, four months

Environmental benefits

It's not my business to guilt-trip parents into trying BLPT for the sake of the environment. The other benefits of BLPT are so striking that I would practise (and advocate) BLPT even if there were no ecological reasons. However, I'm sure you will be glad to know that BLPT also helps the planet.

Whichever way you look at it, nappies aren't good for the environment. In the UK, 95 per cent of parents use disposable nappies,[1] and 8 million are sent to landfill every day (where they can take over 500 years to break down).[2] And nappies containing faeces release harmful greenhouse gases – methane is over 20 times more harmful than carbon dioxide.[3] Eco-disposables are only 'eco' in the manufacturing of the nappy, so they don't reduce landfill. You can lessen your carbon footprint and waste by using washables, but even these have an impact on the environment, especially if you buy new, wash at 60 degrees or use a tumble dryer.

With BLPT, solid waste tends to travel via the potty or toilet to the sewer, where it is treated along with the rest of our waste in a way that won't release methane. And, of course, if baby hasn't soiled or wet a nappy, then it won't need to be replaced with a new one, so BLPT reduces the number of disposable nappies manufactured and sent to landfill, and reduces the amount of laundry if you use washables.

2. An increase in positive parent-child communication

Perhaps the most important outcome of BLPT is the extra bond it helps create between baby and parent. The process opens up a whole new channel of communication, and families are delighted to experience the benefits this brings, which include the following:

Empowerment for parents

It is so easy for an unsettled baby to make us feel powerless – is he hungry? Tired? Overstimulated? With BLPT you get instant feedback: is baby fussing because he needs a poo? – oh, yes, there he goes! This may not sound important, but actually it can be extremely empowering for a parent finding it difficult to understand their baby's cries. And it often turns out that the sensation of a full bladder or bowel is the cause of previously unexplained fussiness. My own son was a rather unsettled baby in his first few weeks, and if he was crying I often found it helpful to hold him in the potty position before I tried anything else. I would get very quick feedback: either he would wee or poo within a few seconds (about half the time), and then he'd calm down, or (the other half) he would let me know *very* clearly that it wasn't what he wanted! And then I would try the next thing on the short checklist – usually a feed. Even when I got it 'wrong', it was useful to be able to rule out a possibility so quickly.

> '*By far one of my favourite benefits of BLPT is that it has demystified what happens in the hidden realms of the nappy. I stopped treating my baby's bottom as a weapon to be 'contained' as quickly and efficiently as possible in a nappy – for fear of pee and poo attack. I got to hold my baby's beautiful bare bottom and let him play as nature intended. I love picking him up, holding him close without worrying. Yes, we get occasional sprinkles, but it's not a big deal and the joy eclipses the moment of wipe up.*'
>
> **Tokozile, mum to Rudy, 11 months**

Confidence for babies

Babies begin to communicate about when they are hungry or tired from birth – and it is well known that this cycle of communication and response between parents and babies helps them develop their language and social and emotional intelligence. However, babies can also communicate about sensations of bladder and bowel fullness, and responding to that leads to more positive interactions with your baby. This kind of effective communication gives babies a growing sense of confidence and also contributes to their language and social skills.

A way to bond

Breastfeeding is often cited as being a wonderful way to bond with your baby, but if it's difficult, it can feel like a conflict at first. It's really important for mums to get the support they need so they can breastfeed as long as they want. In the meantime, BLPT provides an ideal additional (and pain-free) opportunity to bond with your baby. And if you can't breastfeed, either as a mum or a dad, then alternative opportunities for bonding will be even more important. Dads especially can sometimes feel left out or disempowered in the early weeks. BLPT is a great practical way for dads to get involved in baby care. Babies may show just as much satisfaction from a productive trip to the potty as they do after a good feed. This can feel very empowering for dads, especially when the instant feedback shows them they've 'got it right'.

3. More comfort for your baby

It may come as a surprise that, as well as reducing nappy rash, BLPT can help to alleviate other physical discomforts. By helping your baby into the squat position you are literally encouraging his body to perform more effectively. It is far easier to pass waste when in this position, and that can make all the difference between an inconsolable windy baby, and a settled, contented one.

'My baby wasn't gaining enough weight and she was refusing to latch on. I was at my wits' end. My midwife saw her fussing and suggested I hold her in the squat position. She pooped! It turned out that she was ultra-sensitive to the feeling of a full bowel, and couldn't feed properly until she went. Straight away she started gaining weight. I don't know what would have happened if the midwife hadn't suggested holding her like that. Started using formula top-ups, I guess.'

Caroline, mum to Elise, four months

4. Your baby becomes accustomed to using the potty

Further down the line, parents will come to reap the benefits of another unique outcome: your baby will be used to using the potty. This will be extremely helpful when you want to help your child gain toilet independence. The transition is likely to be smoother and possibly earlier with BLPT.

Being accustomed to using the potty (even if only using one occasionally) will mean your baby doesn't need to make that intellectual leap of understanding – *What is the potty for, and how do I put anything in it?* – nor do they find the idea unsettling. Babies will be used to recognising the sensation of a full bladder or bowel. They may even be so used to the potty that 'potty training', or *completion*, is so gradual and seamless a process that it seems to happen all by itself.

You won't need to potty train your child at an arbitrary time, as your child will reach the various milestones in his own time, such as the ability to communicate the need to go in advance, the ability to delay urination for a few moments, the ability to sit on the potty without assistance and the ability to pull down his own trousers. Some of these milestones could be reached as early as a few weeks old; others, such as wiping himself, may take several years. By following your child's natural development, you won't be holding him back, nor will you be putting on too much pressure too early.

Recent studies have also shown that the actual act of using the potty helps to develop the bladder. Scientists found that babies who were already using the potty were more able to fully empty their bladder at nine months than babies who used nappies conventionally.[4,5] Babies who had used the potty also seemed to have better control of their pelvic floor muscles as they had been practising holding and releasing the bladder and bowel from a very young age.

So if the benefits are so great, why doesn't everyone do it?

The recent history of nappy use

Using a potty in babyhood isn't a new idea. Across most of Africa, India, China, and many other countries including in Eastern Europe and South America, parents generally start helping their baby use a potty (or other appropriate place) in the first few weeks and carry on until their baby is toilet independent. In this way, most babies in the world are *out of nappies* by one, and pretty much toilet independent (both day and night) by 18–24 months.[6] We used to do it in this country too. In the UK in 1958, a study of 5,000 mothers found that 85 per cent introduced a potty before six months, and 60 per cent started before one month. (Among professional parents, these statistics were even higher at 91 per cent and 74 per cent).[7] It's probably how your grandmother potty trained your mother.

> *'I used to work with the elderly and when I told them what I did with my sons, they were not surprised as they knew all about it and shared their own stories. It was a nice way to connect with the older generation!'*
>
> **Shyann, mum to Duncan, nine years, and Hamish, four and a half years**

What changed?

Two events in the early 1960s hugely impacted the future of potty training: in 1961 came the invention of Pampers nappies; and in 1962 Dr T. Berry Brazelton published what was to become his seminal 'readiness' paper, advocating a delayed start to potty training.[8]

Brazelton suggested that if parents used 'early reflex compliance' to keep their baby clean and dry in the early months, then it was likely that the child would go through a 'period of lag and breakdown' when the reflexes diminished, but before the child could display voluntary mastery. He was concerned that parents who did not understand about this 'breakdown' of ability (which can occur around 12 months of age) would put too much pressure on their child, leading to stress and regression. In order to avoid this, his answer was to delay toilet training until at least 18 months, when children may have the necessary skill level to manage potty trips by themselves. He felt that 24 months was usually the optimum age for initiation. (I'll explain the different stages your baby will pass through, and specifically about the transition from involuntary to voluntary control in Chapter 2, plus more about the changes in children's pottying abilities in Chapters 10 and 13.)

Brazelton charted the progress of 1,170 children in his practice, most of whom started potty training around 24 months of age, on his advice. Most achieved daytime control within four months. There was no control group of children who started training before 12 months, as would have been typical at the time, and less than 10 per cent of his group started before 18 months, so it's hard to make comparisons. But the study suggested that later training was indeed quick and efficient, and the method quickly grew in popularity. Health professionals have advised parents to follow this method ever since.

Too much pressure?

Because of the advice from health professionals to delay, some parents wonder whether their baby is too young to start potty training and worry that they might put pressure on their baby if they do. The techniques that I advocate are always respectful of babies' needs. BLPT is a very gentle method, where parents and babies work in partnership together. It's certainly not about getting babies to perform, or to reach a certain stage before they are ready. In the past some early-potty-training strategies did use coercive methods, and so starting early got a bad press. This was why Brazelton advocated a delayed approach. BLPT offers another baby-friendly alternative: this time, offering your baby the chance to use a potty from birth, but in a gentle and responsive manner.

Whatever age you practise BLPT, there shouldn't be any pressure on your baby, or, for that matter, on you. As you know your baby best, you should always look to yourself and your baby first when deciding on the right way to do things.

The advent of Pampers

In the years running up to Brazelton's paper, the disposable nappy industry was creating a product that seemed to take much of the work out of traditional nappying. When Victor Mills, who worked for Procter & Gamble, invented Pampers in 1961, the industry really took off. Nappy design was then improved and competition led to lower prices. The next major breakthrough was in the 1980s with the idea to include super-absorbent polymers into the nappy. These were an immediate success as they both reduced the bulkiness of the nappies and increased their absorbency. In developed countries, disposable nappies rapidly grew in popularity, with around 95 per cent of UK babies wearing them by the end of the century.[9]

Looking to increase their market share even further, industry leaders Procter & Gamble saw that delaying potty training would increase sales. In 1983 the company teamed up with Dr Brazelton, and funded a TV show, *What Every Baby Knows*, that he hosted.[10] They also provided funding for his research and projects. Brazelton developed his 'wait until they're ready' approach, which argued that children may not be ready for potty training until aged three or four. Later he became head of the Pampers Parenting Institute and was paid by Procter & Gamble to appear in numerous Pampers commercials.[11]

When Pampers launched their 'size 6' nappy in 1998 (for babies over 35 lbs or 16 kg, which is around aged three to eight years), Brazelton appeared in their TV commercial reminding parents that 'it's got to be his choice!' When asked about this potential conflict of interests, Brazelton told *The New York Times* that he was proud to work with Pampers. 'It took me a long time to decide to do it, but I'm absolutely convinced that it was a wonderful thing to do,' he said. 'I'm certainly not doing it to keep kids in diapers. It's just the opposite: Pampers is willing to go along with me to make it easier for mothers to let kids be open to toilet training when they are ready.'[12]

A trend towards delaying

Subsequent childcare experts, such as baby-centred author Penelope Leach, reinforced Brazelton's advice. In her 1977 and 1988 editions of her book *Baby and Child*, Leach felt that what she called 'potting' (i.e. helping a young baby to use the potty) was popular enough for it to be necessary to advise against it. She suggested that while it is 'harmless enough' at around age seven months, when a baby gets mobile, conflict may arise. (This is indeed something we need to watch out for – I'll tell you how in Chapter 13.)

Baby and Child was the childcare manual my mother referred to when bringing up my sister and I in the late 1970s and early 1980s. I find it really interesting that in the 1950s and 1960s our grandmothers almost universally began potty training before six months. In the 1970s and 1980s, our parents had a hazy notion that it might be possible to catch some of their baby's waste on a potty, but they disparagingly referred to it as 'mother training', as they thought that the method relied solely on hyper-attentiveness combined with lucky timing. By the time we get to the present day, most parents – and even, it seems, most health professionals – *have never even heard* of such a concept, and believe that potty training before 18 months is 'physiologically impossible'.

Nowadays

A recent BabyCenter.com poll of around 25,000 parents shows that 61 per cent of parents start potty training after 24 months, with half of those starting after two and a half years. Of those children who had completed potty training, 38 per cent did not complete until after three years.[13] Although current health advice is based on Brazelton's 'readiness' paper, in fact, many parents are initiating potty training far later than he originally envisioned. Also, I suspect that the parents in Brazelton's 1962 study, who started training from 18 to 24 months, were conscious of how 'late' they were beginning, and so I expect they were very proactive during the training period.

Nowadays, 24 months is considered early, and it is seen as perfectly reasonable to leave training until three. This is up to a year later than the children in Brazelton's 1962 study (which at the time was considered late). Parents are now urged to take a back seat and let their child lead the way. According to the NHS, nine out of ten children are dry in the daytime by 36 months,[14] but it is not unusual to find children still in nappies at age three or even four.

Within two generations, it seems as if we have lost not only the practice of potty training from birth but also the knowledge that the practice *existed*.

The emergence of 'elimination communication' or BLPT

The technique was not to be suppressed for long, however. Just as it seemed that the Western world had completely forgotten how to potty their babies, the method was 'rediscovered' and renamed. Perhaps the most significant pioneer of the method in recent times is the American Laurie Boucke. In 1979 a visitor from India introduced her to the method when her third son was three months old. Boucke wrote numerous books about the subject, including *Infant Potty Training* (2002), and campaigned for its recognition by US health experts. The method spread via the Internet to Europe; though of course, there were families already practising it through intuition, or with knowledge handed down the generations. The BabyCenter poll found that 3 per cent of parents initiate potty training before 12 months, but the numbers are almost certainly higher as many parents who help their babies pass waste would not consider themselves to be 'potty training'.

What's in a name?

Searching for a term that emphasised the partnership and unique bond fostered by the method, Ingrid Bauer coined the terms 'elimination communication' and 'natural infant hygiene' in her book *Diaper Free: The Gentle Wisdom of Natural Infant Hygiene*. These terms, and in particular the elimination communication abbreviation 'EC', were embraced by families in the States. However, some of these terms – 'infant', 'diaper-free', 'elimination' – feel awkward on this side of the Atlantic; I even find 'elimination' a bit sinister! I think that catchy names – especially if they aren't immediately self-explanatory – can give the impression of some kind of club you have to join or identify with. I have known parents to worry if they are 'doing EC properly', or what the 'rules' are (with them questioning 'is this *EC*, or is this *early-start potty training*?'), or even wondering if they are the right kind of people to do EC (Too obsessive? Too pushy? Too lazy?). I don't think that's helpful.

I have instead referred to this method as 'baby-led potty training' (BLPT), as I think that it's the most self-explanatory of the terms. The term 'baby-led' emphasises the fact that you'll be doing a lot of baby watching. The method is about 'tuning in' to your baby, getting to know him better and learning how to communicate on an extra channel. Baby-led *doesn't* mean waiting for your baby to declare he's ready to quit using nappies (as you might expect 'child-led potty training' to mean). It *does* mean responding to your baby's toileting needs at the time they happen. It also means recognising and working with each stage of your baby's development. In the same way that a parent will look for little clues that baby is hungry or tired, you can watch out for when he might need the potty. There will be a fair amount of adult-leading going on too: often parents initiate potty trips according to the clock or convenience, but you can be guided by your baby's body language if it really is the right time for baby. The use of 'potty training' in the term doesn't mean it's all about reaching toilet independence; that will probably be very far from your mind, especially in your baby's first year.

So will my baby be potty trained early?

I can't promise that by following the techniques laid out in this book your baby will be out of nappies at one, with potty training completed by two – as is usual in other parts of the world. That scenario is possible, but it would depend on lots of different factors. (In Chapter 15, I'll discuss why it is more difficult for our babies to complete potty training as early as in some other cultures.) Most importantly, a child can only complete each stage of potty training according to his own developmental readiness. Practising BLPT will enable your child to learn each new skill in his own time, without you having to make a guess whether he is 'ready'. This means that he should reach toilet independence as soon as he is able, rather than at a fixed time initiated by you.

If you decide to use BLPT techniques at night, whether from the beginning, or further down the line, it is *very* likely that your baby will be out of night-time nappies sooner than he would be otherwise. The NHS says we can expect night-time dryness to be learnt between the ages of three and five, with one in six of five year olds wetting the bed.[15] In contrast I have found that parents who practise BLPT at night usually find their children can stay consistently dry at night (either through using the potty, or by holding right through) between one and two years. I'll show you exactly how to achieve this in Chapter 16.

Summary

- You can help your baby to pass waste by holding him in a comfortable position.
- There are many different ways to use BLPT: in conjunction with nappies, as an alternative to conventional nappy use, as a method of potty training or as a tool to soothe discomfort.
- The key outcomes are:
  - Less waste in your baby's nappies
  - An increase in positive parent–child communication
  - More comfort for your baby
  - Baby becomes accustomed to using the potty
- BLPT is used throughout the world, and was standard practice in the UK around 50 or so years ago.
- The invention of disposable nappies in the 1960s, plus the popularity of the 'Brazelton method', led to later and later toilet training.

Chapter 2

The Biology of Toilet Training

Most of us have a notion of what goes on when we urinate and defecate, but I think that it's important to understand exactly what is happening inside your baby's body at different ages and stages, so that you can better understand how to work with him. An incomplete understanding of his capabilities could lead you to expect too much of him – or too little.

The bladder and urinary system

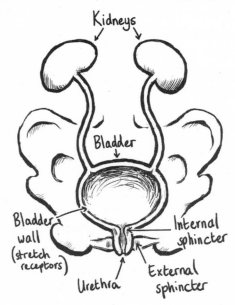

At birth, your baby is already used to urinating; he's been doing it in the uterus for the past five months or so. Blood continually passes through the kidneys in a cleaning process, and urine (the waste liquid) is sent to the bladder, which is around 40 ml (1½ fl oz) at birth. However, it's rare for the bladder to fill to capacity, especially when not in deep sleep. In babies it normally fills up to around 20 ml (½ fl oz) – that's four teaspoons – before alarms start going off.

Signals from the bladder wall go along nerves to the spinal cord, which sends more signals back to the bladder wall to make it contract. But the urine can't get out until both sphincters are open. The first, internal, sphincter is a ring of muscle at the base of the bladder. It's managed entirely by the spinal cord, so we call it an *involuntary* muscle. It opens as the bladder contracts. The second, external, sphincter is a little further down the urethra. This one is a *voluntary* muscle – at least, it's voluntary in older babies, children and adults. That means it is managed by the brain, and it enables us to decide to 'hold' our wee, even when we can feel pressure in our bladder from a contraction and urine has passed through the internal sphincter. We can also decide to open it when we are in a suitable place for urinating. This external sphincter is the important muscle for BLPT. Here are the basic steps of this process:

- Kidneys send urine to bladder
- Bladder fills
- Stretch receptors in bladder wall send signals to the spinal cord
- The spinal cord instructs the bladder wall to contract, and the internal sphincter to open
- The brain keeps the external sphincter closed – momentarily (in newborns) or until a suitable place for urination is reached (in older babies, children and adults)

Many people think that newborn babies have no control over this process; they say that when the bladder fills up to a certain point, the spinal cord instructs the urine to be expelled, and there's nothing anyone can do about that. My experience of pottying babies tells me that the reality is rather different. This is backed up by recent research, which suggests that the process is more complex. Studies have shown that a single baby will empty the bladder with differing volumes of urine. They have also found that babies rarely urinate during naps, especially if they are already using a potty. Both these facts suggest that the brain influences the process, and that capacity is not the only factor.[1]

I have found that even newborn babies express discomfort before urinating, suggesting they can feel a full bladder. It seems that their bladder is contracting and the pressure is increasing, but there is a momentary delay before the external sphincter opens. During this delay they may cry out, squirm or come off the breast. It may be that this delay is due to a disorganisation of the systems, and it takes a moment or two for the body to release the external sphincter. Or it may be simply that this mechanism – the ability of the brain to control the external sphincter, and in particular to keep it *closed* in the first instance of a bladder contraction – is in place from birth, albeit in a rudimentary form. I suspect that, while the process is not *conscious* in the newborn baby, the brain still exerts some control over the external sphincter. Whatever the reason, you can use this delay to your advantage when practising BLPT.

An extremely useful reflex

Newborn babies may pass urine 20 times a day. Regardless of whether they intend to offer a potty or not, mothers everywhere know that removing a newborn's nappy often triggers a reflex to urinate. Holding your baby upright, with his knees above the pelvis further encourages this reflex. Like most other 'primitive' or 'infantile' reflexes it seems to disappear by around four months.

This reflex is a very useful thing for BLPT. It means that with a baby under three months (and sometimes with older ones too), very often all you need to do is hold him out in this squatting position for a wee to appear. Dr T. Berry Brazelton called this 'early reflex compliance'.[2]

Creating a conditioned response

From birth, but most noticeably in the two-to-ten-month period, the sphincter becomes *conditioned* to release in set circumstances.[3] After a few weeks (or even days) of holding your baby out and catching his urine, your baby begins to make an association between the hold, or perhaps the sound, or the feel of the pot on his buttocks (or a combination of these things), and the action of passing urine. This creates a *conditioned response*. If the bladder is full enough, the hold (or other parental cue, which I'll explain later on pages 52–3) can both trigger the bladder wall to contract and instruct the external sphincter to open. This aligns with, and reinforces, their infantile reflexes.

Conditioning takes place, whether you desire it or not. When babies use nappies conventionally, their infantile reflexes fade after a couple of months, to be replaced by a conditioned response to urinate and defecate in their nappies (sometimes waiting until a fresh nappy is put on before urinating).

A baby's conditioned response is not yet a *conscious* decision, but it is managed by the brain. By the time the baby is a few weeks old, this conditioning can be so strong that if baby doesn't feel that he is in the right place, the brain will instruct the external sphincter to remain closed, perhaps for a minute or two or even longer – even when the bladder wall is contracting. The pressure on the bladder increases the baby's discomfort, and he can signal to you that he needs to urinate, giving you time to get him to a suitable place.

Becoming conscious of the sensation

As a baby grows, this process gradually becomes more conscious, and the ability to keep the external sphincter *closed* becomes increasingly under his control. He will begin to easily hold on for a minute or two while you get his clothes undone. Conscious awareness can be displayed in various subtle ways, such as these:

- At four months, he may signal his need to go by, for example, giving you a 'significant look'.
- At six months he may reach out to a nearby potty.
- At nine months he may crawl towards it or make a hand sign.
- At eleven months he may even learn to say 'wee-wee'.

When does voluntary control begin?

Recent research has shown that it is not just the *age* of the child that dictates bladder maturity; studies suggest that *practising* the use of the sphincter, at any age, helps to gain mastery of it.[4] For parents who offer the potty from birth, it can appear as if their babies exert voluntary control almost straight away, as they sometimes seem to 'hold on' until they reach a potty. Keeping the sphincter *closed* is easier than *opening* it, and this skill is learnt much sooner. Babies as young as three or four months may be able to hold their bladders for a minute or two. The process of *opening* the sphincter and releasing the bladder doesn't become truly voluntary for some time, however; instead it is triggered by reflex or *conditioning*.

But even if a baby can't consciously manage the full process just yet, that doesn't stop him being aware that the process *is happening*: even the youngest babies seem to be satisfied and happy about using the potty.

From watching many babies, and my research, it seems 10–14 months (especially the learning-to-walk stage) is a transition period for gaining mastery of the external sphincter. Some children sail through this transition seamlessly, whereas others *appear* to regress in their toileting ability before they gain voluntary control. Typically a baby may show signs of needing a wee, sit on a potty for a minute and then get up without urinating. He may then immediately wee on the floor or in his nappy. In fact he is not regressing, but learning a new skill: voluntary control. The conditioned response is being impeded by the brain, which tells the sphincter to stay shut. A baby can't always work out how to co-ordinate the muscles to open the sphincter, and so nothing happens, and he gets off the potty. Then, when he is at the point of bursting, the external sphincter will open automatically.

Another factor is the 'myelinisation' process: when the brain's neurons are sheathed in 'myelin' – a substance that insulates them and helps information pass more quickly. This process is not completed in this area of the brain until around 12–18 months (with some scientists arguing that full neural control is not in place until three to five years).[5] There are also other factors at play during this stage, which I'll look at in detail in Chapter 13.

It is essential to understand the transition a baby goes through to avoid having unrealistic expectations of your baby's ability during this particular learning period. Brazelton referred to this in his 1962 paper (see page 19) as a 'lag' in a baby's ability to use the potty. From reading historical accounts of mothers potty training their 12 month olds, and even from today's Internet forum posts, it is clear that an incomplete understanding of this transition can lead to frustration on both sides. I think existing resources on BLPT do not pay enough attention to this. If you accept that at some time during the 10–14-month period your baby may take a few weeks to fully master this skill for himself – and have patience as he learns – then you can avoid conflict arising.

It is possible for some babies to reach an acceptable level of toilet independence towards the end of this period, but only if the demands on them are not too high. If they do not have to undo fiddly clothes, and they can get to the potty easily and use it as often as they like, then they may be able to manage toileting for themselves as soon as they are able to walk.[6] In the West, this kind of compliance often depends more on personality type than on physical ability or mental development.

Most Western medical professionals agree that by the age of 18 months children may obtain reasonable control over the external sphincter and can begin to use the bladder as a storage container. When the child learns to hold the bladder 'against' a contraction, the bladder begins to stretch. The typical capacity at 18 months may be 100–150 ml (3½–5 fl oz). This enables him to hold larger quantities of urine, and he will be able to go for longer periods without feeling the urge to wee. He will be more able to hold the bladder, should he need to delay emptying it – for example, in order to reach a toilet.

The bowel

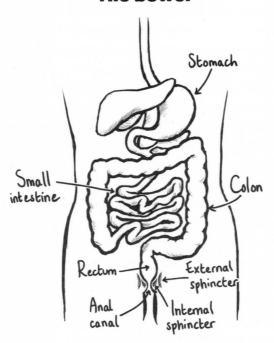

In general, babies don't defecate in the uterus, which means that parents normally witness them pass their first stools of 'meconium' in the first few days after birth. This first poo is strangely black and sticky – the word means, literally, 'like opium juice'. As the baby begins to take in milk over the next few days, the faeces change to be soft – often liquid with 'seeds' – and yellow or orange in colour.

How does the bowel work?

The milk a baby drinks goes into the stomach, where it is met by enzymes and hydrochloric acid. Some water is absorbed at this stage. The matter then passes into the small intestine and is pushed along by a muscular action called peristalsis. Most of the goodness is extracted here. Next comes the colon, where contents may stay for up to 18–24 hours. Only around 4 per cent of the matter, including water, is absorbed from here.

Next a wave of intense contractions push the contents of the colon into the rectum – this 'mass movement' stimulates the urge to defecate. This is often triggered by the gastrocolic reflex, which occurs when the stomach is full. This reflex is a really useful one for BLPT, as it often means you can predict a poo a few minutes after a feed. Pressure receptors in the rectum will then sense the presence of faeces, and the internal sphincter (the ring of muscle that closes the rectum) relaxes, letting a small sample of faeces pass through.

This is the bit that I find fascinating: special nerve endings are able to tell whether this sample is solid faeces, diarrhoea or wind. It's hard to say at what age babies can distinguish this difference. I suspect that babies become conscious of this on some level fairly early, though I have experienced times when generally reliable babies have been taken by surprise by diarrhoea. You can decide for yourself!

In order to defecate, both babies and adults take a deep breath and contract the abdominal muscles which pushes the faecal mass towards the anal canal. The pelvic floor relaxes, allowing faeces to pass through.

Reflexes and conditioning

I've mentioned how air to the nappy area triggers a reflex to urinate; it also seems to relax the external anal sphincter. Parents report that if their young baby goes without a nappy for a few minutes, they often defecate. Because the process takes longer, however, this reflex is not so obvious as with urination. As with passing urine, babies can quickly become conditioned to release their external anal sphincter when they are held in a certain position. We sometimes see them 'trying', even if nothing is produced.

Frequency of stools

Babies will poo very frequently, perhaps three to twelve times a day in the first few weeks, and the stools are often explosive or foamy. Often they just leave a smear in the nappy. The sheer quantity of waste in this period is an advantage to getting started with BLPT, as there are so many opportunities to get 'catches' and start building up an association. The number of poos gradually reduces, and by about two to three months babies usually have around two poos a day.

Resisting the urge

As babies get older, they find out that they don't have to poo every time they feel the urge – it can be resisted by keeping the external sphincter closed. After a while, the rectum relaxes and the need to defecate passes until another mass movement occurs and further faeces enter the rectum.

In many babies, the ability to keep the external sphincter voluntarily closed comes early. These babies may wait until they are on a potty before they release their bowel. They may signal their discomfort in advance, or it may be that the act of sitting on the potty itself (or being held out) triggers the mass movement into the rectum and the resultant urge to defecate. These babies seem to show a preference for the potty as a place to defecate from an early age – and in many cases would meet the criterion for completion of 'bowel training' (as set out by Nathan J. Blum et al., in a 2003 paper in *Pediatrics*,[7] as fewer than two soilings in a month) from as early as three months.

Other babies do not seem to hold back – when the urge comes they indicate their need to pass a bowel movement through either unconscious or conscious signs (see page 62). In this way you can still take your baby to a suitable place in time, so you can similarly keep him reliably clean from a young age.

'We bought a potty when Elliott was six months because he was constipated and I thought that gravity might help him go … So as soon as he woke up, I took him straight to the potty and held him over it. To my absolute astonishment, he did a wee and a poo right then and there. I could not believe my eyes. We usually had to wait a week for a poo to emerge. And there it was: no mess, no fuss. It was like a window had opened up into a parallel universe where babies were not incontinent and ineffectual, but active participants in their own care. I gained a deeper understanding about human nature that day, and have since learnt about other newborn reflexes that we have forgotten about.'

Rosie, mum to Elliott, 23 months

Habits at 12–18 months

I don't think that bowel training usually goes through quite the same kind of 'gap' in skills as we often see with bladder training around the one-year mark, though similar processes are at play, so may affect some babies. However, newfound mobility and autonomy does often result in 'experimentation' in passing stools. It is very common for reliable babies to experiment with pooing in new postures, which were previously unavailable to them – especially standing. This phase normally passes within a few weeks, and your now toddling child will probably be even more reliable than before when it does.

Children in full-time nappies are often observed to go through a similar phase – often choosing to exercise their voluntary control by, for example, going behind the sofa to defecate.

Strong habits at 18–24 months

It is very common for defecating conditioning to start to become entrenched at this age. This means that your toddler may get very attached to pooing in a particular place – perhaps in a particular potty, or at home, or with Dad.

If he is wearing nappies conventionally, it could mean that he becomes so attached to defecating in them that he is unwilling to try anywhere else. This habit may get even stronger past 24 months and cause difficulty potty training. Awareness that his peers are pooing in the toilet may help him to overcome the habit.

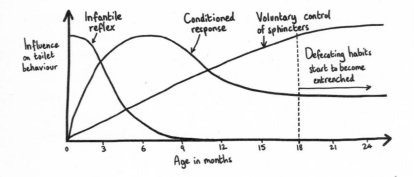

Summary

- Babies up to three months old often wee and poo when their nappy is removed and they are held in a squat position, due to a *reflex*.
- From birth (and especially two to ten months) babies become *conditioned* to pass waste in their regular place. This could be a potty or a nappy.
- The ability to keep the sphincters voluntarily closed begins to be apparent from three or four months.
- The ability to voluntarily *open* them comes later, from 10 to 12 months.
- The baby's brain may learn to override the conditioned response to wee or poo before the baby has fully learnt to *consciously* initiate the process. This may result in apparent 'regression' around the one-year mark.

Chapter 3

When Should I Begin?

The short answer is: now! You and your baby can start reaping benefits from the moment you start holding him over a potty, and the enthusiasm you have when you first learn about the method will help you get started. Generally there is no advantage in delaying, except perhaps in cases where a baby or his parents are ill, or if parents feel they need to focus all of their energy on learning an aspect of baby care such as breastfeeding. In this chapter, I'll talk a little bit about the differences you might find with starting out at different ages and issues you might face if you delay.

When I first started offering workshops in 2008, most of the parents who came had not heard of BLPT when their babies were born. They usually started BLPT as soon as they found out about the method, though some of them waited until after they had been to one of my workshops. In some cases their babies were six months or more, or even 12 months old, but they still had a lot of success with the method.

Because of its growth in popularity, many parents are now finding out about BLPT while pregnant or even earlier. This gives parents an advantage because they can start right from birth.

Starting from birth

If you are lucky enough to know about BLPT in advance, there are lots of advantages to starting directly after birth. The first few days with a new baby are a steep learning curve, as you get used to handling your baby, start learning to feed him and find out how he likes to be held. Even if this is your second or third baby, you still have a lot of learning to do, as each baby is different. If you start holding your baby out in these first few days, then learning BLPT becomes part of the overall process of learning to look after your baby.

The method itself helps you to get to know your baby better. It is difficult to see what is happening in the bottom area when you stick a nappy on a baby straight away, so it is hard to see if his behaviour – crying or wriggling, for example – is related to feeling uncomfortably full. The nappy acts as a sort of voluntary blindfold, which seems very strange when you think that, in pretty much every other respect, you are doing your best to learn what makes your baby tick. It's lovely to be present and helping support your baby when he passes his first bowel movements. Remember, this is an entirely new sensation for him – most babies won't have defecated in the womb so it can be an unsettling process. On a purely practical level, meconium is about the stickiest substance known to humankind, so it's rather helpful if this lands straight in a potty or bowl!

Holding your baby out at this age is likely to result in lots of catches; you can capitalise on the infantile reflexes which will make him wee and poo at predictable times – especially when his nappy is taken off (see pages 28, 29 for more on this). (This reflex will fade over the next few months.) After the first couple of days, newborns tend to pass waste very often, so you will have lots of opportunities to practise, and you may be able to get the hang of the method within a day or two.

I have known a number of parents say that they will wait until their baby is a little older before they start BLPT, as they want to feel more confident with other aspects of baby care first. I can sympathise with this, as many parents feel overwhelmed in the early days. However, in my experience, it is better to start from the beginning. It doesn't have to be much – holding him out once a day, or even once a week, may be enough to start the process. Quite apart from the fact that it's easier to start at the beginning in practical terms (because of the infantile reflex and the sheer amount of waste being passed), I've also noticed that if parents wait it may feel difficult to learn a new skill from scratch, especially once other habits and routines are in place.

> *'Our first catch happened when Pip was only a few hours old. She was on the changing mat and I noticed a tiny droplet of wee and held her straight over a bowl as an experiment ... and she weed!'*
> **Beth, mum to Eva, three years, and Pip, six months**

Starting in hospital

Hospitals have lots of standard procedures for meeting your and your baby's care needs, so it can be difficult to know how and when to initiate a change in routine. The staff will have expectations about how you care for your baby, and they may not be very supportive about different choices, so it may be that hospital is *not* the best place for you to start practising BLPT. Most new mums only stay in hospital for a day or so (or even a few hours), so it may make sense to wait until you get your baby home before whipping out the potty. If you have to stay in hospital due to some kind of complication or illness, then you shouldn't worry about delaying starting for a few days or a couple of weeks, until you feel ready.

However, it may be that it feels right to start BLPT as soon as your baby is born, even in hospital. Perhaps a change in circumstances has led you to hospital when you weren't expecting it. Perhaps this is your second or later child, and BLPT feels so normal that it would feel strange not to do it. Perhaps the nurses are curious and supportive, and you feel encouraged to give it a go. One mum told me a very moving story about how she first built up the courage to try pottying in hospital:

> *'I took my tiny potty to the hospital, but didn't have the confidence to use it for the first couple of nights. It worried me, being a first-time mother, that the staff would see me doing something different*

and either tell me off or think I was a fool and laugh behind my back. But my baby had a terrible night on his second night. He was full of wind and wouldn't settle at all, and at the same time my milk was starting to come in and driving him insane – the feeds I could give him were not yet satisfying enough.

Anyway, the following morning my parents came in and I was in tears, but them being there gave me the confidence to try out the potty. I hadn't really even discussed it with them beforehand, so they looked at me like I was bonkers at first. But I was just explaining the idea, with baby's bum over the potty, when suddenly he did a big poo! And a pee. After that my dad said you could see the relief on his face, and my baby suckled immediately. So my parents were sold then and there.'

Eleanor, mum to Erik, one week

If it does feel right to try your baby on the potty while you are in hospital, then it will be pretty essential to have some kind of potty or bowl with you. You might also find it practical at first to try when someone else is present, so that they can empty the potty for you. Hospitals are normally pretty good for having sinks on hand in each ward, though the nurses may not be too pleased about you disposing of potty contents there!

Starting in the newborn period (2 to 10 weeks)

Starting during this period will hold many of the advantages of starting directly from birth. Babies will still pass waste on reflex when their nappy is taken off, which makes for easy catches. They wee and poo very frequently at this age, perhaps more than 20 times a day, so you will get lots of chances to practise and it will be easy for your baby to make those key associations. It will be impossible to catch all of your baby's waste – but you might expect to catch around half.

Your baby may still be rather unsettled at this age and can be very communicative about his bodily needs. Because he will be unable to make sense of much of the wider world at this age (he can typically only focus at about 30 cm/12 inches), he will be very inward-looking; he will seem extremely interested in what is going on inside his body, and his funny facial expressions reflect this. It is lovely to join him in his world of burps and farts and wees and poos!

> 'We started BLPT on Christmas morning, when my daughter was eight weeks old. After opening the potty, which was a "joke" present from her grandparents, we thought we'd give it a go and held her over it – the joke was on them as she weed straight away.'
>
> **Mel, mum to Emma, 20 months**

Starting from around 10 weeks to 6 months

At this stage, your baby will be holding up his head and may even be able to sit supported on the potty. A lot of cultures round the world wait until this time before they start practising BLPT, so please don't feel that you have missed the boat if you are only beginning now! You may find that you need a little more persistence to get those first few catches to start you off on the process (as babies pass waste less often at this age); however, within a couple of weeks of practice, you and baby will have 'caught up' with families who started from birth. So, while you will have missed out on the day-to-day benefits that you would have gained in the first few weeks, there is no long-term disadvantage.

Those early reflexes will now be starting to be replaced by conditioning: weeing and pooing in the nappy will become your baby's default mode. This is a good time to reverse that trend. Also, he will now be more interested in goings-on *outside* of his body. But I expect that if you hold your baby out a few times a day for a couple of days, you will be well on your way. His less frequent weeing and pooing can also be an advantage – you may find that you are able to catch the majority of your baby's waste. I often think of the three-to-nine-month period as the 'golden age' of BLPT.

Starting from six months to mobile (crawling)

Some cultures traditionally wait until a baby can sit up and is on solids before starting potty training. His early reflexes will have diminished by this stage, so first catches now will need some perseverance. Once you've got started, your baby will be likely to spend more time sitting on the floor, out of your arms. This can be both an advantage and a disadvantage for BLPT; it may seem harder to pick up on his signals now he is that bit further away, but, on the plus side, he will be easier to handle and more settled in himself. He is likely to follow a more predictable routine and may also start to communicate in more conscious ways. Chapter 11 deals with the specifics of starting at this age.

Starting with a mobile (crawling) baby

The mobile baby focuses his attention more on the wider world, and is less receptive to the goings-on inside his body. His early reflexes are likely to have faded, and he will have been conditioned to pass waste in his nappy. This can make this period less suitable for initiating BLPT. On the other hand, he is more able to take an active role in the process. He is also more able to communicate his needs with you. Many parents report great success when starting out in this period, so, although it's better to start earlier, it's still worth giving it a try. The process for starting with mobile babies and toddlers is somewhat different to starting with a younger baby, and I'll explain how to do this in Chapter 11.

Starting with a toddler of 12 to 18 months

The early walking phase is sometimes considered challenging, even for families who have been practising BLPT from birth. Your child will be devoting a huge amount of energy into learning to walk, and he will be less concerned about internal functions. He will be starting to experiment with testing boundaries and asserting his independence. He will also begin to obtain voluntary sphincter control. In the early stages, he'll find it difficult to learn how to co-ordinate this, which can make BLPT more unpredictable. Your toddler will be much more physically able to co-operate in the process and can communicate consciously about it. If you are able to stay patient and have realistic expectations, then a lot can be gained from starting now. However, if you are hoping for quick results, then it might be better to hold off, as it's unlikely he'll be able to complete the process for a few more months. For more on starting during this period, see Chapter 14.

Summary

- The earlier you begin BLPT, the sooner you can start reaping the benefits.
- It's easier to get started with a younger baby, as the method utilises infantile reflexes.
- You can also start with an older baby or a toddler, though you may need a bit more perseverance to get started.

Chapter 4

Getting Started

To get started with BLPT, you have to take your baby's nappy off. It sounds simple, but you will not believe how hard this is for a lot of parents. When I run my workshops I find that even parents who have come specifically to learn BLPT are reluctant to remove their babies' nappies. 'I think he's just about to do a poo,' I hear a mum say. 'I'm just going to give him a feed first.' Or: 'He wees every time I take his nappy off, and it goes everywhere.' 'His poos explode.' It doesn't matter. In fact, if he's just about to do a poo or a wee, this is the best time to take his nappy off. If he's just about to feed, this is a great time. If he does exploding poos – even better! Let's explode them into the potty.

However, I'm not just going to leave you with an exploding baby. Let's go through some of the theory first.

The basic steps to BLPT

There are three key steps to getting started with BLPT:

1. Parents learn how to hold their baby in a squat position and, if the baby is old enough, how to support him on the potty.
2. Parents get the first 'catches' and begin to get a sense of baby's toileting patterns.
3. The baby begins to make an association with the hold/potty and passing waste.

I'll now go through each of these steps in further detail.

Step One: Introducing the potty and the hold

The first step is easy enough – you can learn the basic hold in less than a minute. Your baby 'sits' on your hands, facing away from you. Tilt his knees slightly higher than his pelvis and support his back and head on your tummy or chest.

There are lots of variations of this hold, the most useful of which I'll describe below. This position can be used literally from birth, and for as long as you can still lift your child!

Standing at the sink

One variation is to stand at the sink with your baby facing away from you. You might even be able to smile at each other in the bathroom mirror.

For this hold, you lean your baby's back and head against your chest. Support his weight by holding a thigh in each hand. Draw his knees upwards and outwards and aim his bottom towards the sink. If you feel squeamish about this, put a bowl in the sink first.

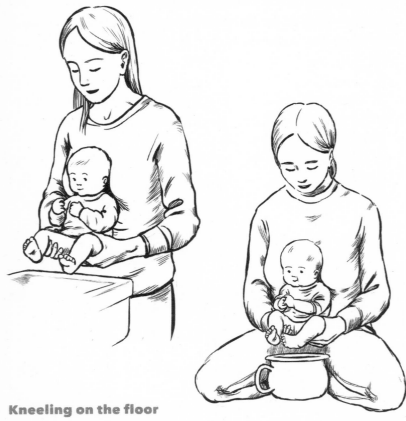

Kneeling on the floor

This position is very similar to the first one, except you may want to hold baby further down your body, with his back resting against your stomach. Unless you are doing this outside, you will need some kind of receptacle to catch the deposit. You can use pretty much anything – ice-cream tubs or Christmas pudding bowls work fine. Just make sure it's deep enough to prevent splash-back. A wide, smooth rim is best too, in case you rest your baby's bottom on it. Some parents even use a nappy, although that defeats the purpose a bit for me. I'll cover more on using potties in Chapter 6.

Over the loo

You can also hold your baby directly over the loo, although this position may be less comfortable for you if you find yourself bending your knees or back. It might be easier for you to sit on a stool or chair. You can also sit right at the back of the toilet, facing forward.

Newborn in-arms

This is another type of hold, which is particularly good with newborns. You support your baby's head in the crook of your arm, with his back supported by your forearm. It is best to use both hands to hold his thighs when he is actually passing waste, but when he is finished you can let go with the free arm (leaving one of his legs dangling) to grab a wipe or splash some water on his bottom. One possible disadvantage to this position is that mums may find their baby gets distracted by her breast.

On the potty

You may find it easier to use a conventional potty with your baby when he has head control, but you'll still need to support his back for a few months. I used a 'toddler' potty with my children from around three months.

There are many different ways to hold your baby; the above are just a few of the classic examples. One Indian grandmother told me that back home they lay babies on the adults' legs, making a kind of potty with their feet. As long as you draw up your baby's knees, and hold him upright so that gravity can get to work, then any position which is comfortable for you and your baby is fine.

Learning how to handle your baby will be one of your first jobs as a parent. It's really important you gain confidence in this, as there will be all sorts of jobs you'll need to do with your baby. He may

Aiming the penis

Some parents worry that boys will spray urine all over the place like an unruly fireman's hose. Certainly boys can produce some spectacular results if they catch you unawares (although girls can produce some pretty powerful jets at times too), but if you are prepared, then, in my experience of both sexes, it is not more difficult to aim a boy compared to a girl. With both boys and girls, if they have a very full bladder, then the stream tends to eject forwards rather than downwards. To counteract this, if you are holding your baby over the toilet or sink, you need to adjust either the angle (lean him forwards a bit more) or the distance (hold him slightly further back).

Depending on the size and shape of your boy's penis and testicles, you may find it helpful to direct his penis. It is possible to do this with your index finger while you support his thigh with the rest of your hand. Some parents use one finger to point the penis down and another to keep the testicles out of the way. Don't be afraid to experiment a little here! I find that the easiest way is to 'dip' a baby's bottom right inside a potty or container, so that his stream hits the wall of the potty. Others prefer to potty boys into something bigger, e.g. a washing-up bowl or the bath or shower.

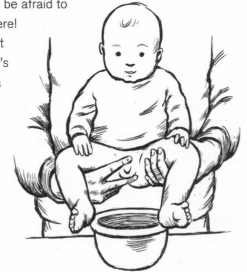

seem fragile, but, in fact, babies are really robust, so don't be scared to pick him up and experiment. You can even do this while he is fully clothed at first.

Step Two: Get some catches and start recognising patterns

The next step is to start getting some catches. This can take more time. Just start offering the potty straight away. You'll need a little bit of luck and also a fair amount of perseverance. Just keep holding your baby out and eventually you will get a catch. Hey, you might even get one the first time you try – lots of parents do, especially with very young babies.

> *'I had my first catch in hospital the day after Skye was born (I had a caesarean). I held her out over a nappy on the bed and caught some meconium and a wee and felt very pleased with myself.'*
>
> **Anna, mum to Harry, three years,**
> **and Skye, four months**

Part of the process of getting catches is starting to learn when your baby is most likely to wee or poo, and what behaviours he displays just before he does.

Some BLPT teachers recommend spending a lot of time observing your baby naked on a mat – perhaps for days or even weeks at a time, before they do anything else. They advise parents to communicate whenever their baby passes waste and to draw the baby's attention to it. This is fine if you want to do it, but in my view it is not very efficient. Spending hours on end watching your baby wee on a changing mat is not the quickest way for a parent and baby to start getting to grips with the method. Much of the time parents may find they miss the critical moment – and for parents with more than one child, it's unlikely they'd have the time for this. I'm pretty sure they don't do this in Africa!

The thinking behind the naked observation time is that you can come to learn what times your baby is likely to go and what little signals he gives off before passing waste. However, I think you can learn these things 'on the job', so to speak. Just make a mental note whenever you notice your baby passing waste (whether a miss or a catch), and see if you can spot any patterns.

Step Three: Allow your baby to build an association

And so we come to the final step. Babies are remarkably clever little creatures. After two or three catches in the potty (whether the sink, loo, bowl or bushes) even a days-old baby starts to make an association between that position and passing waste. The more often you have 'potty success', the stronger the association will get. It is a baby's own natural reflexes, triggered by the squat position (plus the change of temperature or feeling of air), that make him release his bladder and bowel, but the simple fact of the *repetition* of this starts to *condition* your baby to release the pelvic floor as well. This doesn't mean that your baby will wee or poo every time you hold him like this – he has to have a reasonably full bladder or bowel. But you can often see your baby make a little effort, to give it a try.

Some parents find that making a sound can help reinforce the connection – often they make a low whistle or a 'sssss' sound for a wee and a grunting or raspberry sound for a poo. (Blowing a raspberry seems appropriate at first as it mimics the sound of defecation in a young baby; however, it won't be long before the poos stop being explosive, so a grunting noise is probably a better long-term choice.) Some people even use just words as a cue. Parents sometimes ask me if they need separate wee and poo cues at all. I say yes; urinating and defecating are distinct actions, and, at times, it's helpful for your baby to know which one you are referring to.

I'm sure these kinds of verbal cues can help, but in my experience physical cues are much more effective as a prompt – especially the squat hold. This is one of the reasons why I don't think naked observation time (without holding out) is as useful. It's hard for a baby to make an association with just verbal cues – they need physical ones as well. Another physical cue you can give your baby is clenching your own stomach muscles against his back.

One effect of a baby making an association between the hold and passing waste is that he will probably start to hold on to his wee for just a few extra seconds. He will not be capable of using his bladder as a reservoir (i.e. delaying urination for minutes at a time, as an adult can) until at least 18 months or later, but that won't stop him from holding on to a full bladder momentarily until he finds himself in a comfortable position to release it. The sensation of a full bladder is uncomfortable, so if your baby holds his wee for longer than a second or two, you may start to notice him showing the signs of discomfort. This might be wriggling, heavy breathing, crying or kicking his legs. These are the signals that you will start to recognise for when he needs help getting to the potty (see page 60 for more on these signs).

'After reading a thread on Mumsnet about EC, I thought I'd give it a go. I waited for my daughter to wake from a nap, dangled her over the toilet and she weed! We use cloth nappies, and it was great to be able to put a clean nappy back on. We've only been going two weeks now, but she has already started to develop a bit of a special whinge that means she needs to wee – if I hear it and take her to the loo she normally goes straight away. We are using the cueing words 'wee-wee' every time we go, and I try and remember to use the Makaton sign [see page 148] for toilet as well – hopefully she might sign this back eventually.'

Jayne, mum to Ella, 18 weeks

Making use of predictable times

All babies are unique, and parents will get to know their own baby's toilet patterns the more they watch out for them. However, there are some common times that are worth mentioning.

In the morning

Little babies urinate a lot. In the first few weeks, they can wee more than 20 times a day. So there is a good chance you will catch a wee pretty much any time you hold a young baby out. However, I've found that they seem to wee less in the afternoon and much more frequently in the morning, particularly in the first hour after waking. They might wee five times or so in that first hour. In my experience babies tend to gorge themselves on milk just as they are waking up, or at the first feed of the day. Their stomach is capable of holding far more liquid than their bladder (a one-month-old baby has a stomach capacity of around 80–150 ml (3–5 fl oz)[1]), and although some of that liquid will be absorbed in order to meet the needs of cell growth, tears, perspiration, exhalation, etc., the bladder may have to fill and empty a few times to expel the urine. Also, babies tend not to wee when they are asleep – at least not in a deep sleep – so if they have fallen asleep on a stomach full of milk, this will need to be processed as soon as they wake.

On waking

Babies as young as a couple of weeks old may go for two or three hours or more without weeing when they are asleep – for example, during an afternoon nap. So it's good to try holding them out when they wake from a nap.

After being carried in a sling

Babies tend not to wee or poo when they are being carried close to their parent's body in a sling. It seems that when there is pressure against baby's crotch, it is easier for them to hold their bladder, or perhaps, conversely, it is harder for them to release. (We sometimes notice older children sitting on their heel to help them hold their bladder.) I'm sure this physiological effect was not an accident of nature: in evolutionary terms it is very useful for a baby not to wet or soil their parent. I found that when my babies did have a full bladder in the sling, they would give me very clear signals that they wanted to get out: wriggling their legs and crying out. Some babies also prefer not to wee or poo in a reclined position – say in a car seat or bouncy chair – so it's worth offering them a chance to go if they suddenly get fussy in this position, or when you are taking them out after a long journey.

At feeding times

Breastfed babies tend to get bigger quantities of milk right at the beginning of a feed, so it is likely that their bladders will start filling up perhaps 10–15 minutes after that first flush of milk. If your baby has a bottle, it may be easier to gauge how quickly he is drinking, and therefore when he is likely to want to wee. Your baby may wee while feeding; I found that my daughter liked to come off the breast to wee and then go back on, while my son would wait until he'd had enough milk.

Many babies find a full bladder or bowel distracting, and so they will not latch on to the breast or bottle properly in the first place until they have passed waste. Alternatively, they may latch, then fuss and come off and refuse to reattach. It would be typical to find a baby popping on and off the breast or bottle teat in either of these cases. Mums are often advised that if a baby comes off near the beginning of a feed, it is because he needs to burp. It may actually be that he needs to wee instead.

As a full stomach triggers the gastrocolic reflex (which sends a signal to the body to defecate), some families find their baby poos after every feed. It may also mean that a baby poos *during* the feed, as the reflex is triggered before he is finished. Mothers often ask me how they can work around this. It is possible to hold baby over a potty while breastfeeding at the same time, although I would not advise trying this if you are still perfecting breastfeeding, as it can prove to be a distraction for you. Having said that, lots of parents find that opening the nappy during breastfeeding helps them understand some of their baby's previously unexplained behaviours, which may actually help them breastfeed.

To try pottying while breastfeeding, a bit of experimentation is useful. This position may be a bit more tricky when feeding with a bottle, but it is still possible. Hold the potty securely between your legs and position your baby's bottom over it. Then you can use one hand to support your baby and the other to hold the bottle.

Another thing to consider is that if you offer your baby a chance to defecate at some point *before* you feed him, then he will have an empty bowel during the feed, and so won't need to poo during it. Some babies like to suck for comfort while they are pooing, as they find the whole process unsettling; if this is this case, it may be enough to let your baby suck a finger while he goes.

When wiping

When our cat recently had kittens, I was very interested (and rather pleased) to find that we didn't see a single trace of the kittens' faeces until they were on solid cat food at around five weeks. It turns out that the mother licks away all of their faeces. The act of licking stimulates the kittens' anuses and triggers a reflex to defecate. Now I don't recommend that you lick your babies' bottoms (!), but the act of wiping the anus clean can encourage baby to pass more poo.

At change times

Most parents are familiar with the scenario of their baby weeing just as soon as the nappy is off – and parents of boys can get a wee in the face if they are not quick enough with the next nappy! It's worth offering your baby a chance to go as soon as he is naked.

Other good times to offer your baby the potty

- Whenever he is being bathed
- After being in a car seat
- A few minutes after a feed
- If he hasn't weed for an hour or two

I don't mean that you *have* to hold baby out every time you get him out of the sling, or as soon as he wakes up, or any of the other predictable times. But if you are just starting out, then these are the best times to try, as you are most likely to get a catch and your baby will start making a connection.

Essential advice for starting out

When you and your baby are learning BLPT, you will find that the more effort you put in over the first few days, the more progress you will make. Your baby will make the associations a lot faster and the learning will be accumulative. Here are some tips to help you make the best start:

Try frequent offering with observation

With a younger baby, say under two or three months, you can afford to be a bit more random with the frequency with which you offer the potty. However, with a baby older than three months, it will pay to be more consistent over the first few days.

For an older baby, I think it's worth making a commitment to try offering the potty at least six times a day for the first two or three days. If you can couple this with some naked observation time (or with your baby draped in a muslin or terry without a cover), then you will make a lot of progress.

The very best time to set aside for observation and potty time is the first hour of the day, as your baby is very likely to wee a number of times, so you have the best chance of noting his patterns and getting some catches. If you can't put in so much effort for whatever reason – then don't worry! Just go with what you've got. If necessary you can put in a bit more effort later if you feel you need to.

Avoid a mad rush

Sometimes it can seem too difficult to get baby's nappy off in time. Many parents find it hard to get started, because they think that by the time they've got their baby's clothes and nappy off, their baby will have already weed, and they'll have to put it all back on again. This is why I say you've got to take off your baby's nappy to get started. I don't mean your baby has to be naked all the time, but you will need to get over that psychological hurdle of taking off his nappy when you think it might be a good time to try the potty.

It will make life much easier if your baby is not wearing many layers of clothing in the first place. In our house, we banned poppers and dungarees, as we found them just too fiddly. Make it easy for yourself by dressing your baby in easy-access clothes in those first few days when you are learning the ropes. I'll talk more about clothes in Chapter 5.

Experiment with frequency

When you feel confident with the mechanics of holding out your baby and you have a better idea of his patterns, then, if you want, you can

Babies often show their preference

Once you've had a few catches under your belt and your baby has cottoned on to the idea, you may be amazed to find that he can hold on a lot longer than you might have thought. My daughter hated to wee in the car seat, and would make a great fuss if she felt the urge. On one occasion, when she was four months old, we were travelling on the motorway to Cornwall. She started crying and kicking, which we guessed meant she needed a wee, but unfortunately we missed the turn-off for the services. It took us nine minutes to get to the next service station, with her crying on and off all the while. We got her out of the car seat in the car park and put her straight on the potty. Her nappy was still dry, and she did a big wee. We were really amazed that she had held on for so long.

Even a baby as young as two or three weeks can hold on for a few seconds before urinating – easily enough time to get his clothes and nappy off. It's always worth giving your baby the chance to go if you think he needs it, as he may astound you with his holding abilities.

relax a bit with offering the potty. Now is the time to experiment and see what works for your family. Some parents will want to just offer at change times; others will want to step up the frequency and try to catch the majority of waste. And others will want to try to tune in to their baby a bit more and respond more to his own signals.

Learning to spot signals

As you get to know your baby, you will begin to get a sense of the particular signals that he gives to indicate that he needs to use the potty.

Signals for both wees or poos

These are the common signals a baby under six months may give you to indicate a full bladder or bowel:

- **Crying:** This is likely to be the cry of discomfort, rather than distress.
- **Wriggling legs and body:** This is particularly noticeable if he is in the sling.
- **Heavy breathing:** This could be very noticeable or just a subtle change.
- **Fixed stare:** He may look as if he expects you to do something, or he may just have a glazed expression.
- **Popping on and off the breast or bottle:** It might seem that he wants to feed but something is distracting him.
- **Bottom raised up:** When a sleeping baby needs to urinate he may roll onto his front and raise his bottom to take the weight off his bladder.
- **Shivering:** Some babies shiver just before a wee, some shiver during and some, right at the end.
- **A sudden change in behaviour:** This could be anything, but it often catches your attention.
- **Erect penis:** Many boys get an erection a few seconds before they urinate. When I started doing BLPT with my son I was

really surprised at how useful this was. It was more obvious to us in the first three months. Obviously this won't be much use to you if your baby is wearing a nappy, but if he happens to be naked it can be an extremely reliable sign (especially if you are getting your baby weighed at the doctor's!) It's also useful as additional evidence if you think baby needs to go: you take off his nappy, and there it is.

Your baby may display some of these signals and not others, and you will get to learn his own unique ways of communicating.

'Phantom' wee

Another potential signal is an interesting phenomenon that probably has to be experienced to be believed. It most often occurs when baby is in a sling or carrier, or on your hip, with his tummy towards yours, but it can also happen when he is sitting on your lap. What happens is that you suddenly feel the sensation of warmth spreading across your stomach, back or lap and you think that your baby has just weed on you. However, when you take him out of the sling and undo the nappy, you find that his nappy is still dry. Then when you put your baby on the potty he immediately does a wee.

Some people put this down to a psychological effect – some kind of intuition on the part of the parent. But I think that there must be some *physiological* explanation, as it is so striking when it happens. My guess is that there is a rush of blood towards the genital area just before baby wees, and this is the heat that parents can feel. It can occur in both boys and girls. Erections of the penis are presumably due to the same effect: a rush of blood to the genital area.

Signals that indicate poos

A baby may display any of the above signals just before a poo; in fact many parents are unable to tell whether a wee or poo is on its way. This is especially true when babies appear to 'wait' for the potty before they start the process of pooing. I used to find with my daughter that she never specifically signalled for a poo. She had an opportunity to use the potty at least six to eight times a day, and when she was already on the potty weeing she would use the opportunity to empty her bowel too. From the age of around five months she used to give my thumb a squeeze when she wanted to go. With my son, however, I would normally catch him just as he was about to poo: he was already in the act of pushing when I would notice and get him to a potty if I could.

Babies who, like my son, start to pass a stool before making any other signal, tend to display these particular behaviours:

- **Grunting:** This is especially likely if a baby is not doing anything else that might be strenuous or require concentration.
- **Going red in the face:** This signal is fairly foolproof (unless he is about to cry).
- **Passing wind:** This sometimes indicates the need for a wee too.

The benefits of acting on your baby's signals

If you regularly respond to your baby's urination signals by taking him to the potty, something interesting happens: your baby starts to make a new connection – *When I cry with a full bladder, Mummy takes me to the potty*. This then becomes a positive feedback cycle, and your baby's signals, especially the urination ones, will become more and more clear.

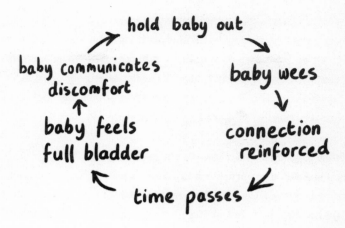

What if you can't spot the signals?

Parents have often told me (sometimes with a tone suggesting inadequacy) that they can't pick up on their baby's urination signals. This stops them from offering the potty.

There are three main reasons why parents are unable to pick up on their baby's urination signals:

1) They are noticing the signals but aren't recognising them

The best way to start picking up on your baby's signals is to make sure you can tell immediately when he is wet. Then you can cast your mind back to see if there were any particular behaviours that he displayed just before weeing. This could mean watching him naked on the change mat, or if you are carrying him about it could mean covering him in just a cloth nappy or muslin so that you can feel when he is wet and warm. Another way is to feel inside his nappy whenever he cries or wriggles about, though this may not be quite so effective. Sometimes it's possible to feel through a disposable the first time a baby wets it, but you would have to be very alert. As mentioned before, you don't have to do this observation time *before* you try holding your baby out – a combination of both is ideal.

Lisa and Mark found that their two-week-old baby would often cry sharply during sleep. They found that she would settle back to sleep after they rocked her. Once they started to observe her without a nappy on, they found that the sharp cry signalled a need to urinate. The rocking seemed to soothe her, but it wasn't actually helping their little girl to relieve herself.

2) The signals are diminishing

This reason is more common in babies who are two months or older and are new to BLPT. Most newborn babies give clear unconscious signals when they are weeing, as they are very absorbed in their own bodily sensations. However, if you don't respond to the signals because you don't know what they mean, by default the feedback you give is that weeing (especially) is not interesting and can safely be ignored. These signals will start to diminish as a baby gets used to his bodily sensations and becomes less interested in his body and more interested in the outside world. In cases where a baby doesn't seem to make any signal at all, then you will need to build up the association between the potty or squat hold and urination first. You will need to do this through timing, intuition and a bit of luck and perseverance. Once your baby makes this association and starts to hold his bladder a bit, you are likely to find that he starts making signals (although you might find that he only does this once he has decided he prefers the potty). See page 145 for more on disappearing signals and how you can encourage your baby to start signalling.

3) Some babies just don't signal at all

All babies have periods when they don't signal. This may be a prolonged period of a few weeks or months, or it might be just a single wee in the afternoon which passes without comment from your baby. Both scenarios are completely normal.

If your baby still doesn't seem to signal after you have explored the previous two reasons, then you may find that you will have to work with just timing and intuition, instead of signals. It may be that he is not inclined to hold his bladder at all at this age, and so doesn't ever feel any discomfort. This is no bad thing, so please don't worry.

Some parents find a similar thing with feeding, especially if they pay attention to a feeding routine. They may find that their baby doesn't signal much for hunger because the parents pre-empt that need by providing a snack/meal or milk at the right time. If parents offer the potty regularly, the sudden urge for a wee can also be pre-empted, so your baby might not get used to signalling for a full bladder. That's not a problem; in fact it can be quite convenient for everyone concerned.

'I found that my baby wouldn't clearly signal for wees at all – I understand some babies do, but not all. So we do all our BLPT (for wees) using timing, and for poos a lot is timing too.'

Emma, mum to Marie, 10 months

Troubleshooting

'My baby screams every time I take his nappy off'

Most newborns cry when they are changed or undressed. This can be a real knock to confidence for new parents. It can put them off having skin-to-skin time with their babies; it can make them nervous of bathing and changing them; and it can also deter parents from offering the potty. For many newborns, the problem is that they dislike being put down. My son was like this. He liked to be held up close, pretty much constantly, for the first few weeks. I found that it helped if I changed him in my arms, or on my lap. He was also calmer when he had something to suck. He still didn't like to be undressed.

After a while, babies get used to the sensation of being handled. It helps if you can stay calm yourself and use soothing words and touch. It's tempting to just rush through and get any changing or undressing done as quickly as possible, but that won't help your baby learn to get used to it. Another trick is to dress him in clothes which don't require much adjustment – a nightdress or 'bundler' can be useful as you don't need to undo any poppers to get to the nappy.

If your baby seems to be crying every time you hold him in the potty position, then it may be wise to take a break from offering for a while, as it is quite possible that he could build up a negative association here. You could wait a couple of weeks until your baby is more settled and start offering the potty then. Having said that, your baby may be crying over the sensation of a full bladder or bowel, so holding him as he cries might be the best thing to do. You will have to apply a lot of trial and error in these situations. You are bound to get it wrong sometimes – often there is no 'right' answer.

'My baby wees every time I take his nappy off and it goes everywhere'

This is a great sign! It means your baby has a healthy trigger reflex. You can use this to your advantage to get started with BLPT. The trick is to be ready with the potty/sink/loo the moment you take his nappy off. It's easier if you remove his nappy while he is in your arms. You can do the first part on the change table – checking there is no poo in there – and then, while the nappy is still loosely in place, but not fixed, you can scoop him up and position him for the potty. Let the nappy fall away and, hey presto: he can wee to his heart's content! Once he has got the hang of using the potty/weeing in that position, he probably won't wee as soon as his nappy is off but will learn to wait a moment or two for you to get him into position.

'I know he needs to wee sometimes, but he is asleep and snuggling in my sling – I don't want to disturb him'

I started BLPT from birth with my son. In the early days he would spend a lot of time snuggled up in my stretchy wrap sling. Sometimes he would make an uncomfortable noise, and wriggle around a bit, but he hadn't actually woken up. At such times, I was pretty sure that he had a full bladder. *What should I do?* I wondered. *Should I wrench him out of the sling, where he is all warm and snuggly, or should I let him wriggle around for a while and wee in his nappy?* When faced with this situation, it is a good idea to recall why you are offering the potty, and then weigh up the pros and cons of offering. If you want to reduce laundry, and/or save nappies at all costs, or if your baby is suffering from a severe case of nappy rash, then taking him out of the sling for a wee may well be the best course of action. Or, if he is wriggling around every 10 minutes, unable to settle into a deep sleep, it may be kinder to help him wee, so he can sleep in comfort. However, at other times, it might make more sense to leave him be.

On many occasions, I found that my son was happy enough to either put up with the full bladder and go back to sleep for a full 45-minute cycle, or he would just go ahead and wee in his nappy. Sometimes I was busy with my eldest child, or in a building where I couldn't potty him. (I'll talk more about pottying when out and about in Chapter 6.) If I wanted him to stay in the sling, I would try to help him relax and wee into his nappy by grasping his thighs through the fabric, and whispering 'pssss' while he slept. For me, the benefit of practising this method was not always using fewer nappies, or the cleanliness, but the increased communication and understanding. If I hadn't known why he was suddenly squirming and uncomfortable, I may have, for example, taken him out for a breastfeed, or simply felt stressed and started rocking him.

This particular dilemma is very likely to disappear with time. An older baby of three months or more is much less likely to wee while he is in the sling. His bladder is bigger and he is able to hold on for longer periods. The position itself discourages the release of the pelvic floor. Also, he is less likely to wee in his sleep, due to the increase in the hormone vasopressin (for more on this, see Chapters 7 and 16). If he does really need to go, he'll often make such a fuss that it is clear the best course of action is to take him out of the sling without further ado.

'I just can't seem to get any catches'

When you start BLPT with a newborn it seems as if you only need to hold him out to get an instant catch. But, as the weeks pass, your baby will start to wee less often so, if you start later, you may find it harder to get those first few catches. That doesn't mean you are failing, or you aren't 'in tune' with your baby – he probably isn't signalling much. By default he will have become conditioned to wee in his nappy, so he may even be 'holding on' when you put him over the potty. You just need a little bit of perseverance and a little bit of luck. It will happen.

I suggest that you mark out a day and really try to make a catch more likely. Choose times when your baby is likely to go – immediately on waking, before and after feeds, when coming out of the sling or car seat, etc. Give him enough time to relax. Prepare for success by dressing him in easy-access clothes. You could aim to hold him out around eight times in the course of the day. I would be surprised if you didn't get a catch before the end of the day. It doesn't take a baby long to catch on to what's required, so you should soon be well on your way. Check that doubt is not holding you back from really giving it your best shot.

'I think my baby needs to poo, but when I hold him out, nothing happens. He then goes as soon as I put him down'

There could be two things going on here. Firstly, it may be that you are not holding your baby out for long enough. Sometimes it does take babies a minute or two (or more) to relax and co-ordinate the muscles needed to expel a bowel movement. Make sure you are in a comfortable position yourself, and just keep holding your baby unless he starts to complain. If he is relaxed and happy, there is no need to give up holding him just because you think it may have been too long. (Although if your arms are getting tired, or you have to switch off the oven, that's another matter.)

Secondly, it could be that your baby has become conditioned to going in a different way – for example, while lying on his back, or while wearing a nappy. Babies can make associations for poo, and start exercising their preferences, surprisingly quickly. Even from two or three months, your baby may start to show almost complete bowel control. If he has made an association to go in the 'wrong' place, you may need to gently break that association. Don't worry; he won't be psychologically attached to anywhere in particular at this age – it's just that his body may have become conditioned to one place or another. If so, it may take him a little longer to relax in what feels like an unusual position to go in.

Persevere. If you suspect your baby is about to pass a bowel movement (perhaps he is farting, going red in the face or grunting), then take off his nappy and keep it off. Keep trying him on the potty or holding him out, and hopefully you will soon catch something. If not, you may need to wait until he is actually in the process of pooing and quickly transfer him, so the majority lands in the potty. This is actually a very effective way of 'retraining' him, though you may need to keep a close eye on him and act fast!

'My baby cries loudly just before he wees'

In my experience babies around two to three months of age, who are used to the potty, often make a sharp cry just at the moment that they are weeing. I think that this is because they have built up some control of their bladder and pelvic floor muscles and they momentarily hold a wee against a contraction of the bladder. The sensation of having a full bladder and then releasing is a short but sometimes intense discomfort. It's worth taking the time to observe this sensation in your own body. We adults have got so used to the sensation that we barely notice it. Babies, however, are experiencing it for the first time, and they may find it uncomfortable and disconcerting – hence they cry out. Any discomfort ought to disperse the moment the wee is released. This stage of crying out doesn't last long: babies quickly get used to the sensation.

If you think your baby is in pain, rather than just alarmed, however, you should take him to the doctor to check for a urinary tract infection. (And you can amaze your doctor by providing a urine sample. GPs sometimes even suggest *syringing* a baby's bladder due to the perceived difficulty in obtaining a clean sample.)

Summary

- There are three steps to getting started:
  1. Hold your baby upright with his back on your chest. Draw his knees up higher than his pelvis. This position relaxes the pelvic floor and encourages him to pass waste.
  2. Keep holding your baby like this until you catch some wees or poos in the potty. Start to notice patterns in timings and his behaviour just before going.
  3. Your baby will begin to make an association between passing waste and the hold, and may start to show a preference for the potty.
- Babies tend to wee or poo at predictable times, e.g. on waking or after a feed. They also display signs of discomfort when they need to go, e.g. crying, heavy breathing, wriggling or kicking. Offering the potty at these times means that you are more likely to get a catch, and your baby will build up an association more quickly.
- Associations lead to a preference for the potty, which means your baby is more likely to signal his need to go.

Chapter 5

Nappies and Clothing

Using nappies or not

The idea of raising a baby nappy free is one that seems to fascinate and boggle. Parents sometimes try to conceptualise a nappy-free baby and get stuck. 'But how …?' they start to ask. They imagine themselves, their carpets and their furniture covered in excrement and they go no further in exploring the method. If the idea of having your baby go nappyless for all, or part, of the day, fills you with terror, then don't worry, because you can do BLPT in conjunction with nappies.

Nappy free life in Asia and Africa

Throughout much of Asia and Africa (particularly in rural areas), babies are generally nappy free. Practising BLPT is a way of life for these families, and in some places having a baby in nappies is seen as lazy parenting. In general, BLPT techniques are very effective at managing babies' waste. But, even so, misses are still an inherent part of the process. The fact is, in cultures where BLPT is the norm, society in general is much less bothered by the odd puddle or occasional poo. Flooring and climate has a fair amount to do with it: half of the world's population live in a dwelling with an earth floor; and warmer weather leads to fewer clothes and easier drying. In the West, misses may be more problematic. Quite apart from the fact that they can cause more work in practical terms (cleaning up the carpet, for example), our culture is also much more squeamish about bodily functions.

A practical approach to nappies

When you practise BLPT, it's completely up to you whether you want to use nappies and, if so, how much and in what manner.

Some parents set out to practise BLPT with a very clear idea about how they want to handle nappies (whether for or against), especially when they have had to decide what to buy during pregnancy. I don't think this is a particularly helpful approach. Ideally, I think it is better to get a feel for the method, and then use nappies, or have nappy-free periods, according to what seems practical at the time. My preference was for whatever led to the least hassle (although I'd also take into account how my choices would affect my aims). Sometimes for me this meant my babies wearing a nappy to minimise the washing of clothes. At other times, especially if I felt the odds of a miss were low, it meant leaving their nappies off for a while because I couldn't be bothered to go upstairs to fetch a new one.

Most parents who practise BLPT, even those who do it all the time, do still use nappies. However, instead of letting their babies wet and soil them indiscriminately, they use the nappy as a 'backup' – just in case of a miss. This means that when they are offering the potty, a single nappy may last a whole day. (They may also have periods when they use a nappy conventionally too.) The more comfortable you get with the method, the more likely you are to 'risk' nappy-free time. It's quite likely this will happen without you even realising it: you've just caught a big wee and then you cuddle and play with your baby for a few minutes before you put his nappy back on. Or, maybe you discover a miss in his nappy while you are out, and you forgot to bring any spares, so you just 'wing it' nappy-free style for the rest of your outing. In my opinion, this kind of casual attitude is one of the great joys of the method.

'For me the best part is the fact that Rafi is, and has been, nappy free so much of the time. I have always felt that nappies hinder the natural movement of the babies' legs, and it's lovely to see him

moving about completely freely. I know not everyone does it like that but that's a big part of it for me.'

Juliet, mum to Luca, 4½ years, and Rafi, 17 months

'I can keep my baby clean and dry all of the time when we are at home without having to use nappies. I think she is far more comfy that way. I don't like the idea of my baby sitting in a waterproof cover all the time with a humid environment (or sitting in her own wee) around her bottom – that doesn't seem hygienic or healthy to me at all.'

Emma, mum to Marie, 10 months

More nappy-free time as your baby grows

Your choice of nappy-free time will also probably be influenced by your baby's age and stage of development. I found that while my babies were in the in-arms phase, and particularly during the first few weeks, using a nappy as backup for most of the time made a lot of sense. Daily misses were inevitable, so wearing a nappy saved on washing. However, once they started to be a bit more independent and played on the floor, and especially once they were crawling, I didn't bother with a nappy as much when I was at home. Soon after my daughter was walking, I found that it was more convenient for her to wear pants, as they were easier to pull down. We'd still often get a miss, but a small one, so changing trousers or tights wasn't any more difficult than changing a nappy.

It's important to prioritise the practical side of things, but it's also necessary to consider how nappies and clothing will influence your approach to BLPT.

Clothing and nappies as an obstacle

There is no doubt about it: the type of clothes and nappies your baby wears will affect *your* behaviour. Parents often ask whether their baby will be able to hold on long enough for them to undress him. The short answer is: yes, he can. At least, certainly after the first few catches. Babies can easily wait the 20 or so seconds it will take to undress him. He can probably wait a minute or two. However, lots of complicated clothing layers can cause problems in BLPT. In the following example you can see how more layers quickly equates to more misses.

Sarah is just learning the ropes of BLPT. She is holding her baby in her arms while sitting at the computer. Her baby has started fussing and squirming for no apparent reason. It occurs to her that this might be a toilet signal. Perhaps she should try him on the potty. She considers what she'll have to do.

To get to his bottom she'll have to pull off his booties, snap off six poppers on his dungarees, six poppers on his babygro, three poppers on his vest and four poppers on his nappy (that's 19 in total!) She'll pull the clothes away from his legs and bottom and unfasten his nappy. She doesn't have a potty yet so she'll have to run up the stairs to the bathroom. She'll hold him over the loo. He probably wouldn't want to go, or she will have already missed it, she thinks. Then, once she's tried him she'll probably need to change his nappy. Then she'll refasten all of those 19 poppers (much more fiddly than unsnapping them) and pull his booties back on. Finally she'll go back downstairs to the computer.

Or, instead of doing that, she might find it more tempting to try rocking him for a couple of minutes to see if he settles down. She'll be changing him anyway in a few minutes, after she's finished this email.

You can see that her baby's clothes are a mental obstacle for Sarah in this example. In reality, if Sarah did in fact bite the bullet and try her baby on the loo, she may well find that he does a wee and a poo and so save herself the bother of changing his nappy a few minutes later.

The problem is that the *hassle* of the clothing is coupled with the *doubt* she has about the method (or her own ability to read her baby's signals.) Together they lead to hesitation. And, once we start to hesitate, the chance of a catch falls by the second – or so it seems.

In contrast, Charlotte, in the following example, has prepared herself for success by making things as easy as possible:

> Charlotte is also sitting at her computer with her baby in her arms. He cries and she suspects it could be a toilet signal. She's just learning the ropes. He's wearing a T-shirt, a jumper and thick long socks. The only thing he has over his bottom and penis is a clean, folded muslin square, tucked up under his T-shirt front and back. He also has a blanket over him, as it's a little bit chilly today. Still sitting in her chair, she reaches for the bowl that's next to the computer. She wedges it between her legs, and then pulls off the blanket and the muslin. She slightly adjusts her baby's position so his penis is aimed into the bowl. He does a wee and a poo. When she's sure he's finished, she reaches for a wipe from the desk to clean his bum – there's only a speck. She wipes her hands, puts the bowl on the desk and the muslin back into place, and pulls the blanket back over him. Then she carries on with her email. She'll clean out the potty when she's finished.

Charlotte is not just sitting watching her naked baby, but she has prepared the environment to help her to respond easily to possible signals. Her baby is only wearing a muslin, so she knows through touch that he is still dry and clean. She might not know for sure if he needs the potty, but if she doesn't try him, she risks him wetting the muslin, which probably won't contain everything. She has made things easy for herself by having the bowl and wipes to hand, so she can just reach out for them when she needs to. Because there is not a single popper between her baby's bottom and potty, the hassle of removing and rearranging his clothes is minimal.

In fact, this is a carrot-and-stick method – the carrot is the hope that she will get a catch, and the stick is that Charlotte risks wee, or worse, soaking through the muslin. Some parents don't find the stick helpful, and so they would prefer to have their baby in more foolproof backup – an open disposable, for example.

If she keeps this up for a couple of days, Charlotte is likely to pick up her baby's signals, and help him make that association a lot faster than Sarah. Once she is more confident in her ability to respond to her baby, it's not so important what he wears. Lots of layers are still a hassle, but it's really *the doubt* that stops you trying it out. When Charlotte is confident that she can read her baby's signals, or she knows that it is a good time to try the potty, she won't let the poppers get in the way.

Which nappy?

For many parents, the choices surrounding nappies are bewildering and sometimes emotive – even before you've factored in the added complication of BLPT. The fact is that you can do BLPT whatever nappy your baby is (or is not) wearing. However, just as with the clothing that baby wears, the type of nappy will make a difference to the way you practise the method. In some cases the effect is psychological, in others it is more practical. I'll explore and assess the different choices now.

Disposables

Most people use disposable nappies, and you can certainly use them for BLPT. I used a mixture of disposable and cloth nappies as backups with both my children. Disposables are actually pretty good for BLPT in the sense that they are easy to undo and refasten. (Some brands, and even some batches, are better for resealing than others.) One of the advantages of disposables is that you don't necessarily have to change a wet nappy – they always feel dry to the touch. When my son was small and would poo more often than wee, I sometimes put in a disposable nappy liner (more commonly used for cloth nappies).

That way, if he just did a little poo in his nappy, I could toss out that soiled liner, and reuse the disposable. A halfway house option is to use purpose-made waterproof covers where you can put in a disposable insert or a cloth one.

If you are using disposables, just be aware that you may need to put in a bit more effort to stay motivated. It can be all too tempting to put off a potty trip – especially if you are just starting and have doubts. I don't recommend them for the initial learning period; it's better to have your baby naked or wrapped up in a muslin or towel if you don't have any purpose-made cloth nappies to hand. But once you have got the hang of the method, then disposables can work fine. I know some parents who used disposables but found that, when BLPT was going well, they were reusing the same nappy for so long that the sticky tabs would give up before the nappy got wet. Or they found they were throwing away clean disposables at the end of the day. If you are finding that to be the case, it may make financial sense to switch to cloth nappies or even cloth training pants. They are a lot more durable than a disposable nappy!

'We have always used disposables, which was pretty unconventional for BLPT. I always worried that it would affect his awareness but I just wasn't willing to put myself through the stress of cloth (as it would have been for me!) Incidentally, at 16 months I was given cloth nappies and decided it was time to use them as I didn't want Toby's awareness of weeing to be non-existent and it was right about that time that he started saying "wee-wee" or "poo-poo" when he needed to go. I don't know if it was just coincidence or if wearing cloth helped him, but it certainly was a great move. In the end he was only in cloth nappies for two months before he switched to wearing pants. Cloth nappies can seem so daunting in the midst of all the other baby chaos, and I'm pleased to report that using disposables for so long didn't seem to affect us negatively.'

Jill, mum to Toby, 20 months

Cloth nappies

In many respects cloth nappies are more suited to BLPT, but the choice can be bewildering. When choosing a type of cloth nappy for BLPT, there are three main things to consider:

1. How easy is it to remove and put back on?
2. How quickly will you notice if your baby is wet?
3. Does it motivate you to respond immediately?

1) How easy is it to remove and put back on?

Most nappies on the market are pretty similar in terms of how easy they are to get on and off. Velcro is slightly easier than poppers but can lose its stick over time and may chafe mobile babies. Avoid nappies with ties and also two-part systems, normally called 'shaped nappies', which need to be fastened on both the absorbent layer and the waterproof layer (unless you are just using the absorbent layer – in which case they can be useful).

If you are looking for a nappy that will reliably protect against leakage for at least one missed wee, but the ease of removal and replacement is top priority, then perhaps the very best type of nappy is a purpose-made 'drop-flap' nappy. This kind of nappy has a waistband that stays on the baby, but when you take him to the potty you unfasten or untuck a 'flap' that drops down, revealing the genital area. The absorbent element is a removable insert that is easy to change if wet. To make the best use of this type of nappy, your baby would need

to be wearing it with chaps, split-crotch trousers, long socks or baby leg warmers (more about these clothes later), as it would lose much of its usefulness under a pair of ordinary trousers.

2) How quickly will you notice if your baby is wet?

The other thing to consider is how the nappy system helps or hinders your awareness of your baby's toileting patterns. In general, any system that includes a waterproof element (all conventional nappy systems) will make it harder to check whether your baby is dry or wet. Of course you can see and feel a wee instantly if your baby is naked from the waist down, but this may not be practical, especially if you are holding him. A good halfway house is using something absorbent that will feel wet straight away. In general, the rule is that the more likely a cloth nappy is to contain leakage, the harder it is to get on and off your baby. (This isn't the case for disposable nappies, which are easier to get on and off than cloth with poppers, but they provide less awareness as they always feel dry.)

3) Does it motivate you to respond immediately?

The other thing to consider is whether a less absorbent nappy will motivate you to respond more quickly (in case of leakages) or not. In general, if a baby is wearing cloth, parents are more inclined to act on signals or misses, as they tend to dislike the idea of their baby sitting in a wet nappy (whereas disposables or cloth with a stay-dry fleece liner, always feel dry to the touch). However, this can sometimes work the other way: before I had decided to make life easier for myself and choose potty-training-friendly clothes, I recall times when I put off pottying my daughter. I suspected a miss, but didn't want to go to the hassle of changing her cloth nappy at that moment. I preferred to stick my head in the sand, so to speak. Had she been wearing a disposable, I might have pottied her, knowing that I could reseal the same nappy, even if there was a wee miss in it. You need to explore how this works for you.

Reducing your laundry pile

In the early days, when a baby is weeing a lot and parents are trying to keep aware by checking his nappy, then dirty nappies are bound to pile up. This stage will pass! A few weeks after you start, you will probably find that you are using substantially fewer nappies. However, in the meantime, you can take steps to cut down the laundry pile:

1) You can use a stay-dry liner so you don't have to change wet nappies every time. These liners can either be disposable paper liners or soft fleece. The fleece is a more effective moisture barrier but it needs to be washed if soiled. The disadvantage of using liners is that it may make it hard for you to keep in touch with what's going on in your baby's nappy.

2) You can use smaller nappies. For example, if you are using some kind of prefold or terry nappy, you could cut each one in half (or buy/make smaller ones). This means that you would double your stash without increasing the weight of your laundry pile. You'll still get through as many nappies, but you won't be running out or washing as often.

3) Don't wash the nappies in the machine. If they are wet, you could just give them a rinse and hang them straight on the line or radiator. Because little baby wee seems to dry away to nothing anyway (without smell or stain), a friend of mine used to just hang them up on the line − wee and all.

4) 'Recycle' used burp cloths or even sicky clothes as nappies. Just pull them out of the laundry basket and fold them into the nappy. He's only going to wee on them, so it doesn't matter if they aren't perfectly clean!

For some parents, having their baby naked will make them ultra-conscious of their baby's signals. This could be helpful or unhelpful. You'll need to find the right balance for your own level of sensitivity. When my son was toddling, I found that I was happier cleaning up the floor than a nappy, so having him naked *reduced* my motivation to potty him. (That worked well for us at the time, as I was trying to let him have more autonomy.)

Extra considerations

There are some other things to consider as well – some of which are specific to BLPT and some that are relevant for all cloth nappy users:

- **How bulky is the nappy?** This will have some impact on how much freedom of movement your baby has, how his clothes fit and also how much room the nappies take up in the wash. It is actually quite good for young babies' hip development to have their hips opened wide by a bulky nappy, though the same effect can be achieved by carrying them in a good sling. (If babies have a serious hip problem they may need to wear a cast.)
- **Is the nappy durable?** Sometimes the waterproofing qualities of the polyurethane laminate (PUL) layer degrade over time and after lots of washes. This will have more impact on all-in-one nappies or pocket nappies, as once the waterproofing has gone the whole nappy will need to be thrown away, whereas if the cover and the absorbent elements are separate, then the absorbent part can be saved. Some nappies are elasticated round the waist and can be pulled up and down like pants. This can make potty trips easier, although you won't really see this advantage until your baby has enough strength in his back muscles for there to be something for you to 'pull against' – also, it's easier to pull down when your baby is standing up by himself.

Weighing up the options

Below is a list of nappy backup options to accompany BLPT. The list goes in order from those giving most awareness and least protection to those giving the least awareness and the most protection. The top five may not provide 100 per cent protection from leakage; you may find that this creates unnecessary stress, or it may add useful extra motivation. This is something to explore.

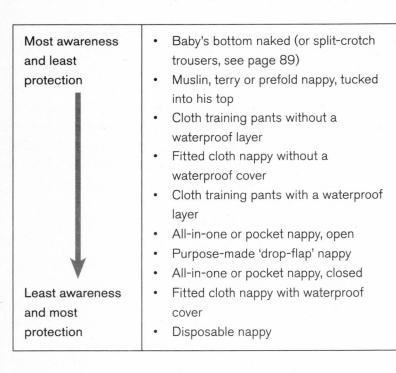

Most awareness and least protection	• Baby's bottom naked (or split-crotch trousers, see page 89)
	• Muslin, terry or prefold nappy, tucked into his top
	• Cloth training pants without a waterproof layer
	• Fitted cloth nappy without a waterproof cover
	• Cloth training pants with a waterproof layer
	• All-in-one or pocket nappy, open
	• Purpose-made 'drop-flap' nappy
	• All-in-one or pocket nappy, closed
Least awareness and most protection	• Fitted cloth nappy with waterproof cover
	• Disposable nappy

I am not saying that the system at the top of the list is best for BLPT and the bottom is the worst. They just have different functions and effects on behaviour, so it's good to be aware of those. I think that all of these options have their place within the practice of BLPT. I have certainly used all of these different methods. I found it unhelpful to have the pressure of possible leakage during my daughter's first year, but with my son I was more confident and laid back, and misses didn't worry me, so I found the practical advantages of no nappy at times outweighed the threat of leakage.

A pragmatic approach

You will probably find that how you nappy your baby will be down to many different factors: how full the washing basket is; whether the in-laws are coming; if you really want to focus on your baby's signals; or if you are on the school run with older children. Experiment a bit and find the right balance for you. It will probably change from day to day and week to week.

> 'As I have problems with anxiety and depression, at times I just felt too overwhelmed (although perhaps everyone has days like this!) I couldn't cope with lots of misses so I would just put him in a nappy for an easier life and so I could get on with chores without interruptions. On the flip side, our regular potty times have been a lovely way to take time out, chill and read stories. They have been a little oasis in our day.'
>
> **Charlotte, mum to Zephyr, 18 months**

I've used lots of different nappy systems as I tend to use a mix of hand-me-down cloth nappies from other people, with a few of my own designs thrown in. I really like low-tech solutions, so most of my nappies were in fact muslin squares, or small squares of cut-up towel that I folded up into a waterproof cover. I did this from when my babies were tiny, right through until we stopped using nappies. I kept them really small – during the day I only needed enough absorbency for one wee miss – so, although I had lots of them, 30 of them hardly took up any more space in the wash than say 10 really thick, absorbent nappies. Having lots of small nappies meant that I was significantly more relaxed about misses. Another advantage of using squares of towelling or flat 'prefold' nappies is that they are very versatile; they are great for mopping up misses on the floor, or for spreading out under my baby on the change mat or in bed. They dry much quicker than shaped nappies.

I don't think there is any perfect nappy solution. My advice would be to get hold of a selection of different systems and use whatever seems right at the time. Different systems will suit different ages and stages of development.

How many nappies do you need?

What I will advise with nappies is: get lots! In order to use cloth round the clock, the cloth nappy websites say that you need around 20–25 nappies. However, with BLPT you would be better off having 30 or more. I think that the more nappies you have, the less stressed you will feel about misses, and it's really important to stay relaxed about that, as misses are an inherent part of the process.

If you are using a two-part nappy system, such as with prefolds, terries or muslin squares inside a cover, it's good to have more *inserts* than conventional cloth users (i.e. 30 or more). You can often get away with fewer *covers* as they are less likely to get soiled; you might need three or four, rather than the six or more you'd use for traditional nappying.

With disposables, although you don't need to plan ahead in the same way as you might with cloth, you may still like to have an idea of how many nappies you will get through in the early weeks. This will vary greatly according to three factors: 1) how often your baby poos; 2) how much waste you are catching in the potty; and 3) how you feel about your baby lying in a wet nappy. If you are catching lots of waste, and you are happy for him to be in a wet nappy between potty trips, you may get away with six nappies or fewer per day. This will reduce further as your baby gets older. However, if he soils his nappy very frequently, then you'll need to change more often. And if you like your baby to be in a dry nappy between potty trips, you could be looking at 10 or more nappies a day, in the early weeks.

Will you use fewer nappies with BLPT?

One of the big outcomes of this method is that more of your baby's waste will end up going down the drain. This means, of course, that less waste will end up in his nappy. The following example shows how this can lead to fewer nappies used.

> For the purposes of comparison, let's say that Karolina and Eva both have babies of six weeks old. On Monday both of their babies poo eight times, with a wee each time too, and they wee (only) a further eight times.
>
> Karolina uses disposables conventionally. On Monday she changed every soiled nappy and also a wet nappy first thing in the morning and after her baby's bath. She used 10 nappies over the course of 24 hours.
>
> Eva is doing BLPT along with disposables. On Monday she caught six poos (along with a wee each time) and a further three wees. She had two poo misses, which she changed each time, and she changed one of the five wee misses. That's three nappy changes altogether.
>
> We can see that BLPT has led to considerable savings on conventional disposable use for Eva.

However, it doesn't directly follow that BLPT means you will be using fewer nappies on any one particular day. This is especially the case if you use cloth nappies, and you like to change your baby immediately after a miss.

> Let's say that Leema and Marie both have three-month-old babies who poo twice a day and wee 15 times.
>
> Leema uses cloth nappies conventionally, and on Monday she changed the two soiled nappies, plus changed her baby's wet nappies another three times. She got through five nappies in total.

Marie uses cloth nappies in conjunction with BLPT. On Monday, Marie caught both of the poos and eight of the wees. As soon as she discovered they were wet, she changed the seven wet nappies.

So, despite the fact that she does BLPT, Marie ended up using two more cloth nappies on Monday than Leema. However, Marie found the washing easier, as she did not have to deal with any soiled nappies.

The likelihood is that once you have got the hang of BLPT, and especially during the 'golden period' of three to nine months, you may only get through one to three wet nappies a day. However, there will be some days, especially at the start, when you may have 10 or more misses a day.

Do you need to change every miss?

I sometimes hear people say that when you practise BLPT, you *have* to change each nappy as soon as it becomes wet. Laurie Boucke, author of *Infant Potty Training*, argues that getting used to wet nappies makes potty training harder. I'm not convinced about this, as most babies seem utterly oblivious to a wet nappy. It's best to draw attention to the miss in some way or other, though this doesn't necessarily mean a fresh nappy: you should do what you feel most comfortable with.

I did tend to change my daughter straight away, but with my son there were many occasions when I left him in a wet nappy, in particular at night and on long car journeys. If I could predict those times, I used a disposable or a cloth nappy with a stay-dry liner. Having a selection of nappies that can be used for different situations could be the best solution. In particular, it's useful if you can vary the absorbency of the nappy, for example by adding more inserts.

Clothing choices

I've talked a lot about nappies here. But the choice of clothes that a baby wears over the nappies is equally important for BLPT.

The fact is that a lot of clothes made for UK babies aren't particularly suitable for the purposes of BLPT. It is most likely that you will already have a cupboard full of babygros, vests, snowsuits and dungarees. You probably have lots of cute outfits for your baby that you are looking forward to dressing him in. That's fine – I'm not suggesting that you need to throw out his current wardrobe. As I've said before, once your baby has learned the ropes, he should be able to hold on for as long as it takes for you to undress him.

However, for the learning period, I strongly advise that you make things easy for yourself. Set aside some time (whether a few hours, a few days or a couple of weeks) when you are committed to focusing on the method. This doesn't mean that you'll be staring at your baby the whole time – I just mean that you'll make a decision in advance to offer the potty at appropriate times, and you'll dress him accordingly.

Helpful conventional clothes

The key to dressing for success is easy access to the bottom, or the nappy if he is wearing one. You probably have plenty of clothes that will allow for this in your cupboard.

If you are at home, and it's not so important how your baby looks, then good choices are long socks that pull right up to the thighs. If your baby has big thighs, then his big brother's or dad's will do. Or you can buy long 'welly' socks for two year olds. (It's possible to buy special stretchy devices that go round the foot and heel to keep babies' socks in place.) T-shirts and jumpers without poppers work well. Some people find that dungarees with the leg poppers undone work for them. For girls, skirts and dresses are an obvious choice. I made my son a kilt!

If you are heading out of doors, and your baby needs to look a little more presentable or be a bit warmer, then tights (for boys too), leggings and tracksuit bottoms can also work well. It might be harder to spot misses, but they are easy to pull up and down.

Aren't poppers designed for easy access?

Certainly dungarees or snowsuits (for example) with poppers are better than those without any access at all. However, while poppers might be quick to undo, they are certainly not quick to do up. As I have said before, it is not the time it takes you to undress your baby that hinders BLPT – babies can easily hold on for that length of time –it's *the doubt* in your mind that causes an obstacle. The thought of having to redo 15 poppers on a wriggling baby can be enough to put you off trying. Also it's practically impossible to do this task away from the change table, or other similar surface. Ideally, when learning BLPT, you can offer your baby the potty or loo in any room with minimum fuss. The idea of then having to take him to the change table turns the procedure into a bigger job than it needs to be.

Purpose-made clothes

Of course, in other cultures and in this country in times past, clothes were designed with easy access in mind. Until the early 20th century, it was standard practice in England for young boys to wear dresses or gowns. 'Breeching', when boys were allowed to give up their skirts and don trousers or breeches, became a rite of passage, once toilet training was safely completed.[1] In more recent times, trousers for babies and toddlers often had a flap at the back to give access to the nappy. In warmer temperatures babies may be carried about naked, but many parents will have to account for the cold – and the carpets!

Chinese split-crotch trousers

BLPT is the norm in China, where it can be extremely cold, and the designs of their baby clothes reflect both the fact that babies need to stay warm and that parents need to have easy access to their bottoms. Most babies and toddlers in China wear split-crotch trousers called *kaidangku*. These are often trousers sewn with a double seam along the crotch; parents cut the crotch to make a slit. Alternatively, they are bought pre-cut and hemmed.

Older babies and toddlers in China don't wear any kind of nappy. For much of the time the split stays closed, but when the toddler squats, or the parent holds the baby in a squat position, the split opens up and the bottom can be directed towards the right place. Parents of very little babies sometimes tuck a prefold-type nappy into the trousers to guard against misses.

In extremely cold climates, for example in Siberia, the children may wear two pairs of trousers: the first pair has the traditional split and the outer pair is like a standard pair of trousers. When the child needs to go, they can pull down the 'normal' trousers, and keep the split ones on while they squat, to keep out the cold. It's possible to import these trousers from China, and there are also a growing number of businesses in the UK and US specialising in them. (I keep an updated list of some of these stockists on my website: www.nappyfreebaby.co.uk.) The most useful types are made from either pure wool or polyester fleece, as both of these fabrics repel liquid. Wool can also be 'lanolised' to make it more waterproof. This is a process you can do at home by adding lanolin (an oil that comes from sheep's wool) to the fabric. This means that they don't absorb much of the wee that comes into contact with them and don't have to be washed for every miss. With my son, I used these trousers most of the time. Some were made by a friend; others I cobbled together myself out of the sleeves of old wool jumpers.

I think that in China it is often seen as acceptable (or even preferable) to allow a baby's genitals to be somewhat exposed to the cold air – just as we might consider it acceptable for a baby's head and hands to be uncovered in cool weather, while in other countries, such as Spain or Mexico, parents do not. However, I think most UK parents would hesitate to allow their baby's genitals to be open to winter frosts. And we may get a few raised eyebrows too! I felt happy about using these trousers by themselves when we were at home (with a normal T-shirt/jumpers, socks, etc.), but if it was cold or we were going out, I would normally put on a cloth nappy *over the top* of the trousers. This worked for us because at the time we were catching most bowel movements. It was very easy to remove the nappy to offer him a chance to use the potty. If we had a wee miss, then the cloth insert would absorb the urine and the trousers would remain dry.

I appreciate that not everyone wants to dress their baby in this way. Whenever my washing would allow, I tried to use matching colours or fabrics so that the split-crotch trouser/nappy combination wouldn't look too much like something Superman would wear. But, as I said before – you don't have to use special clothes. You need to find a balance between making things easier for yourself and making use of your baby's existing clothes. You can think of it as similar to breastfeeding. Most breastfeeding mothers in the UK find it useful to wear a purpose-made breastfeeding bra. You can also buy tailor-made nursing tops and dresses with hidden splits and flaps. Or you can adapt your existing clothing to work around breastfeeding. It isn't sensible to wear a dress that zips at the back, for example, when you are just learning to breastfeed.

Other useful clothes

Wool 'longies' are another useful clothing item. These are like leggings that have waterproofing qualities because they are made of wool. In days gone by, these were knitted in preparation for the new baby. They can be useful as you can just tuck in a prefold or use a cloth-shaped nappy inside, and you don't need an extra waterproof layer on the nappy. Baby leg warmers are another BLPT favourite.

Summary

- It's your choice whether you want to use a nappy as a backup or not, and, if so, what type to use. What a baby wears on his bottom half may influence how you offer the potty, but it doesn't dictate it.
- BLPT can help you use fewer nappies, but it depends on how you respond to misses.
- Layers and poppers between you and your baby's bottom contribute to *doubt* and *hesitation*, which are big hindrances to BLPT. To make life easier for yourself, you can adapt your baby's existing wardrobe, or you can use specialist clothes.

- Helpful clothes for BLPT are:
  - o Stretchy elastic waistbands (tights and tracksuit bottoms)
  - o Skirts and dresses or kilts
  - o Long socks or baby leg warmers (instead of trousers)
  - o Split-crotch trousers
- Unhelpful clothes are:
  - o Many layers
  - o Babygros
  - o Poppered vests
  - o Poppers in general

Chapter 6

Day-to-day Practicalities of BLPT

Once you and baby have got the hang of BLPT, you'll start to get a feel for how often holding him out is right for your family. This may change from day to day or week to week. That's fine, as BLPT is very flexible. At some point in your baby's second year, you'll probably want to take a more consistent approach, in the lead-up to toilet independence, but I'll address that in Chapter 15. For now, it's no problem if you want to limit offering the potty to just mornings, or when you are at home, or at each nappy change, for example. Your baby will take it all in his stride. Alternatively you may find that you want to concentrate on BLPT for a few weeks, and then later the technique might slip into the background, while you and your baby focus on other things.

In this chapter I'll be discussing the practical details of incorporating BLPT into your daily life. That doesn't mean you need to offer the potty in all the situations I describe. At first it's best to take things slowly, and see what you feel comfortable with. And if you do decide you want to take things further on one particular day, that doesn't mean you have to do it again the next. It is fair to say, however, that the more consistent you are with offering the potty, the more likely you are to become 'tuned in' to your baby, which will result in more catches and fewer misses or 'false potties' (when you offer baby the chance to use the potty, but he doesn't need to go). If you offer the potty more haphazardly, then the 'catch rate' is likely to be more patchy too. This is not to say that you *should* be more consistent. You just need to get a feel for what works best for you.

Using potties and other receptacles

It's possible to do BLPT without a potty – if you really prefer not to use one. You can hold your baby straight over the loo or one of the variety of places I mention in this chapter. However, I definitely recommend also having the use of a potty or some kind of bowl, because it makes life a lot easier. Potties are designed to be portable, so you don't have to keep jumping up to go to the bathroom each time your baby needs to pass waste. Even if you are just at home, it is very convenient to keep a potty nearby. It means, for example, that you don't even need to get off the sofa to help your baby use the potty.

Having a potty nearby helps to overcome the twin obstacles of doubt and hesitation – the two enemies of BLPT! Also, as baby gets older, he may not like to interrupt his play. With a potty, you can bring it to wherever he is playing, which will be less disruptive for him. Older babies also like using a potty because they can learn how to climb on (and off) by themselves. This promotes independence and can make it more fun and attractive for them. I think it's worth having two or three potties in different parts of the house. And one at Grandma's too!

With babies under four months

Normally the most important thing with little babies is that you can hold the potty or bowl steady between your legs. It's best if the container is big enough so that you can 'dip' his bottom into it and deep enough to prevent splash-back. A wide rim or lip is also more comfortable for a baby's bottom, though it is possible to hover him just above. Many household containers will serve this purpose: some kind of bowl such as a mixing bowl or a large Christmas pudding bowl can work, or a Tupperware or ice cream tub might do. Look out for children's beach buckets too – many of them are ideal for BLPT.

There is a potty on the market designed specifically for young babies, which looks rather like a plastic top hat. Parents report that it is more suitable for girls, as the opening is not always big enough to dip in a boy to prevent splash-back. I think that a far superior option is an authentic Victorian-style children's chamber pot. Enamel ones are very hard-wearing; they have a sturdy handle, which is useful for holding at night and also for attaching to rucksacks when travelling or out and about. They are also designed in such a way that they don't spill if they are knocked over. On my website, www.nappyfreebaby. co.uk, you can find an up-to-date list of stockists of potties and other useful equipment.

With babies over three or four months

Once your baby can sit, either with support or independently, then you can progress to a toddler potty. Choose one that is nice and low with a wide base and a wide seat. It's worth buying a quality one that will withstand being thrown around and climbed on; it's likely to take a few knocks over the next couple of years! Also, it can be helpful if you are able to tell whether or not there is a deposit in the potty without disturbing your baby. There are some transparent potties on the market, or with some potties you can squeeze your hand underneath it and feel if the bowl is warm.

Potty chairs are also very good for providing a safe, cosy place for your baby to sit. However, these are normally higher, and your baby will probably take longer to learn how to climb on to this independently, compared to a low potty.

With older baby boys, you should watch out: sometimes, if they sit too far forward, boys can catch their penis on the seat of the potty as they sit down. If they wee like this, they'll make a puddle on the floor. This is more of a problem with older babies and toddlers. As you help him on to the potty, double-check his willy is inside the potty, and when he is old enough you can encourage him to start checking this for himself.

Cleaning up the potty

The one drag about potties is emptying them. However, putting off emptying your potty isn't as problematic as putting off a toilet trip. I found that, in the early days, a potty might get used more than once before it gets emptied. That's not a big deal unless there are older siblings or pets racing around.

To dispose of the contents, simply pour the contents into the loo, and swill the potty with water. A bit of toilet roll can wipe out any poo residue. If your potty is really well used, then little scratches inside the bowl can get discoloured. I found that scrubbing it with toilet cleaner every now and again got it looking fresh again.

Where to use your potty

It's best to keep your options open and use a variety of places for your baby to empty his bladder or bowel. It's natural for babies to get attached to going in a certain place, with a certain person or on a certain potty. That's because they have built up a strong association. This is especially true of poos. If you think about it, you will probably find that you have an attachment to doing your business in a certain place too! Portaloos, squat toilets and cubicles without a lock, for example, can make us feel uneasy. Of course, you need your baby to have some association – that's how the whole method works – but it will be much more convenient for you (and your baby) if he connects weeing and pooing in a range of different places. It can also prevent problems with holding bowel movements later on.

Other places to 'go'

Straight down the drain

It also makes a lot of sense sometimes to hold your baby straight over the loo – for example, if the potty is not nearby and you have to get up off the sofa anyway, or if he is just about to have a bath. In which case, you won't have to do any clean-up at all – just flush!

It's also possible to hold your baby over the sink. Urine and even bowel movements in the early days are sterile, so this isn't as unhygienic as it sounds. Now, some people are *very* squeamish about this – that's fine; you don't have to do it! The sink is a good option as it is at just the right height for holding your baby without bending over, and there is often a mirror so you can smile at your baby. Then the taps are very handy to splash his bottom clean and wash away the offering. If you like those advantages but you don't want your baby to wee or poo straight in the sink, you could put a bowl in first. I felt comfortable pottying my babies into the sink while they were exclusively breastfed. Once they began eating solids (which affects both stools and urine), I stopped using the sink and stuck to the loo and potty instead.

> *'I used to use a bowl or a potty, but after a while I realised straight over the toilet (and now sitting on the toilet) is a whole lot less messy.'*
>
> **Beth, mum to Eva, three years, and Pip, six months**

Straight in the garden

Babies and toddlers really love weeing in the garden. The fresh air, the sights and the sounds seem to relax babies and help them to wee quickly. I used to distract my son with a leafy branch while I held him out. It might even be that the cooler air to their bottoms may trigger a reflex to urinate. (Perhaps we have actually evolved with a preference for outdoor weeing, as it was useful to avoid urinating in the prehistoric cave.) Whatever the reason, babies really seem to love it – so it's a great card to have up your sleeve if you think he needs the loo but is having trouble relaxing indoors. I even offer this choice in winter. They will only be outside for a few seconds, and the cold air seems to help them go.

Out and about

The thought of offering the potty when out and about can be daunting, so it's completely fine to use nappies conventionally for outings and just offer the potty at home if you prefer. However, I've often found outings more straightforward than pottying at home. And if you have a baby who signals his need to use the bathroom very strongly, you may find it hard not to respond. I think the idea of pottying when out is harder to grasp for parents with their first baby. Parents with older children tend to be very used to factoring in toilet trips, so it doesn't seem so strange to take baby when he needs to go too.

Adjusting to a new idea of need

With a first baby there can be a sense that taking your baby to the toilet on outings is somehow inappropriate. One mother told me a story from when her baby was three months old: her mother-in-law, the baby's grandmother, had invited the family to stay and they were planning a trip to a craft show. The grandmother wasn't familiar with the idea of offering such a young baby the potty, and she was concerned that the method was making too much work.

'Surely you won't bother with taking her to the toilet, when we are at the *craft show*, will you?' she asked her daughter-in-law.

The grandmother was worried that special trips to the toilet would be inconvenient for everybody in the party. There also seemed to be a sense that the mother was going a bit 'over the top' in her parenting, and that putting her baby's 'need' to go to the toilet over the convenience of the adults in the group was somehow pandering to the baby too much.

Now, the grandmother can be forgiven for this attitude. From her perspective, every other baby happily and unconcernedly wees and poos in their nappy without any kind of to-do. And grandmothers in particular can find it hard to accept practices in childcare that differ from their own. To this grandmother, it would have seemed strange and overzealous to whisk the baby off to the loo, when she would have been perfectly happy to wee right where she was. The grandmother would also have found it harder to recognise and interpret baby's expressions.

However, if the situation was slightly different, and it was the baby's *father* who needed to relieve himself at the craft show, or an *older sister*, then the grandmother wouldn't dream of suggesting that they wee in their pants right where they were. Likewise, if baby was beginning to cry for a feed, then the party would find somewhere to sit down so she could have some milk. And if the baby was getting tired and needing a nap, then the party would have to accommodate that too – either with the baby in a sling, or in a pram, or back home to bed. The difference in this situation is that the grandmother doesn't recognise a toilet trip as a *need*. In this particular case, the mother was able to recognise her baby's communication that she needed to urinate, and knew that in general her baby would be more comfortable being held out in an appropriate place.

Is it a *need*?

That's up to you to decide! As I said before, you don't have to take your baby to the toilet when you go out. Yes, it can be more inconvenient to potty your baby on outings, so you need to decide whether the benefits of pottying him outweigh the inconvenience. This will probably change from moment to moment. As a rough rule of thumb, I only used to take my babies to the loo or other suitable place when out and about if either:

1. It was convenient for me (for example, if I were going to the loo myself or changing my baby)

2. If my baby was signalling a need to go to the toilet very
   clearly – for example, if my daughter was in the sling she
   would start crying and wriggling

My babies hated the feeling of a full bladder when they were in
the sling and didn't like weeing in there either, so when they
signalled a need to me when I was out and about, I would 'drop
everything' and strive to find a suitable place to potty them.
Some might suggest this created undue inconvenience. And perhaps
– if I hadn't encouraged them to signal – my babies might have
learnt to stay quiet, and I could continue shopping. Or they might
have cried but I wouldn't have a clue why. But I didn't mind taking
them to the toilet. In my experience, the only time offering the potty
becomes a chore is when there is an element of doubt – *does he really
need to go?* When my babies signalled in the sling, I was 100 per
cent sure they wanted to go, so I didn't have a problem rising to the
occasion.

These moments can make lasting memories:

> *'I remember discovering that my son's jumping in the sling during
> walks was when he needed a wee, and being brave enough to try
> our first out-of-the-house wee in our local woods at about four
> months, I think.'*
>
> **Hanna, mum to Alex, three and a half years**

Minimising inconvenience
So let's assume that you are open to the idea of offering the potty (or
toilet) when you are out and about. Now I'm going to look at how we
can make that as easy as possible.

Pre-empting the need
Perhaps one of the simplest ways of keeping things convenient and
manageable for yourself is to pre-empt your baby's need to urinate.

In practice, this means offering him a chance to use the toilet at a time when it is convenient for you. For example, you could offer the potty just before you leave the house to go out, when you arrive somewhere, or when you go to the loo yourself.

Once you are well established with BLPT you will probably have an idea about how often your baby wees at various times throughout the day. When my babies were older than about three months, they would tend to last for a couple of hours in the afternoon without needing to wee. So if they went to the loo just before leaving the house, I knew I had a couple of hours to play with. Transitional moments, especially when baby is coming out of a sling, car seat or pram, are typical times for baby to urinate anyway. These are often convenient times for you too, as it is often easier to visit a toilet just on arrival or on departure.

Finding public loos

Generally it's not too hard to find a toilet in a town centre. A number of shops have loos or baby-change and feeding areas, although sometimes there is a code to open the door. In our town there are customer loos in Boots, Marks & Spencer, BHS, Mothercare, Debenhams and in the town hall; there are also a couple of council-run public loos, though these are more grimy. Once you start offering your baby the chance to go on outings, you'll get to know the location of the toilets in your local area pretty quickly. Virtually every single café, restaurant or pub also has a toilet, and I find that if you ask politely and show your baby, staff are more than happy to let you use their loo.

> *'My tip would be not being scared of trying BLPT outside the house. We have always used nappies when out but actually our catch rate is better than at home and it's surprisingly easy to do, even if you don't carry a potty with you.'*
>
> **Kathryn, mum to Natasha, 10 months**

Carrying a potty or toilet insert

Sometimes, despite our best intentions to keep a variety, babies can get particular about where and how they wee. It is quite typical for babies to go through a phase of not wanting to be held in your arms or even supported at all. This can be difficult when you are in a public loo. One way of getting around this is to bring a potty or toilet insert with you. You can buy a great little contraption which is perfect for these situations: it is a small fold-up potty, which can also open out to be a toilet insert. When used as a potty, it has a disposable plastic bag with an absorbent pad inside to catch the offering. This is no worse than using a disposable nappy, but I preferred to use mine in conjunction with a small take-away tub underneath. There's generally somewhere appropriate to empty it.

If you're far from a toilet

I have often heard parents say, 'I knew he needed a wee, but I was miles away from the nearest loo.' If you are in the middle of town, and there is no appropriate place to potty your baby in the immediate vicinity, then it may seem futile to try to get him to the nearest toilet. However, if you are prepared to make the effort, then your baby may well astound you with his holding capabilities. There have been many occasions when I have had to take a baby along a street, through a shopping mall, up an escalator, wait in a queue for a couple of minutes and finally get my baby out of the sling and undressed to find he/she still had a dry nappy and a full bladder.

It's worth trying to get your baby to the potty if he is signalling, especially if he is in the sling – he will find it uncomfortable to wee in this position, and presumably the pressure on his crotch makes it easy for him to hold on. Do tell him you are trying to get him to a toilet. If you get there and find he has already weed, then still offer; he may learn that it's worth holding on for a little longer.

If there are no toilets - in a built-up area

You may find yourself in an urban area with no loos around. Some people say it is fine for a baby to wee anywhere a dog can wee. Personally, I didn't feel comfortable weeing my babies on to plain tarmac. (Unless it was raining – that seemed to make a difference with me!) In general I tried to find a patch of grass or a tree or bush for my baby to wee against. Failing that, I would use a storm drain. I'm sure some people find it offensive to see a parent weeing a baby on to a public space, so I would try to be discreet. If I had a potty with me, I was happy for my baby to sit on it openly. Even if I then poured the contents of the potty into a drain or at the bottom of a tree, somehow I felt this was less offensive than weeing my baby directly on to the tree. I have also been known to sit my baby on the potty in a shopping centre or train station (though not in a café or library). I tried to be aware of other people's perspectives but, ultimately, I tended to put my baby's need to go over the possibility of offending strangers. You need to decide for yourself what you feel comfortable with.

If there are no toilets - in the countryside

If I was in a park or in the countryside, then I felt comfortable about helping my baby wee on a tree or bush. It is very common to see potty-training toddlers doing this! I avoided playgrounds or other well-used areas. I used to find that my children tended to poo at home, so it was not often that I had to deal with an unexpected poo. On the odd occasion when a poo appeared, I would normally remove it with a bag or tissues or nappies – whatever I had to hand. If it was a breast-milk poo, and I was off the beaten track, then I might consider burying it. It was normally possible for me to tell before my son pooed, so I was able to quickly slip something in the landing zone to catch it. Alternatively, if your baby tends to poo often or with little warning, or if you are expecting a poo to arrive soon – for example, because it's the morning and he normally poos first thing – then bring a potty or Tupperware out with you.

When at other people's houses

This really depends on whose house it is, and your relationship with the owner. In general, it's easy enough to take your baby to someone's bathroom. However, if you are enjoying a good natter with your friend, you would probably find it more convenient to have a potty to hand, so you don't have to leave the room to try your baby on the potty. Ask their permission first; some people are a bit funny about bodily functions – and we should respect that in their house. You may also feel comfortable using a potty in the main room at a mother-and-baby or toddler group. I have often seen parents openly potty their babies at La Leche League meetings, for example.

When at someone else's house, your baby should be wearing a nappy between his potty visits, or at least something that guarantees protection against a puddle – e.g. training pants or thick trousers. I have learnt from experience that some people take a very dim view of wee on their floor! I have only one friend where we had a reciprocal arrangement that it was fine for our babies to wee on each other's floors. With all the rest (including Grandma's) my babies wore a nappy.

In the car

Some babies are happy to wee and poo in the car, but others find the reclining position uncomfortable. It's a good idea to keep some sort of potty in the car – especially if you are going on a long trip. My daughter was always very clear when she wanted a loo break – she would start crying and fussing. As I mentioned before, on one occasion on the motorway, at four months, she held on for nine minutes before we could find somewhere to stop. Depending on the type of potty, you may be able to remain seated yourself, with the potty between your legs and your baby held in place over your lap. With a toddler potty, you'll probably need to get out of the car and sit the potty on the seat. Alternatively, I know parents who have their babies use the potty in the boot of the car. Of course, it's normally also possible for a baby to wee out of doors, but the potty option will be warmer in winter, and more discreet.

On trains, planes and coaches

My favourite kinds of transport come with their own loo! However, sometimes babies and toddlers (and, let's face it, even some adults) can be a bit funny about using rattling train loos, and it's not always that easy for the parent to manage all the paraphernalia and keep their balance. This gets increasingly difficult once you have two or more children to squeeze into the cubicle. I find it easiest to use a potty at my seat, and then empty it. Again, the Victorian type of potty with a handle is perfect for this kind of situation.

> *'It's amazing how easy it is to get a baby to wee in an aeroplane toilet. I don't think we had a single wet nappy in our eight-hour flight to the Caribbean!'*
>
> **Alastair and Michelle, parents to Iris, four years, and Gabriel, six months**

When you can't go

Sometimes, it really isn't possible to give baby a chance to use the toilet. This might be because the needs of your other children don't allow for it or because you are 'trapped' in a place where you can't use a potty (or don't have one). This has happened to me lots of times – on the bus, for example. I would try to prevent this scenario by pre-empting with a potty trip before we started, but it didn't always work out. It's important to ensure your baby is wearing an effective backup nappy in these scenarios.

I have found that the best way to deal with this situation is to talk to your baby, acknowledging his need to wee. You can try holding him in the squat position, with his nappy on, to help him wee in comfort. Once I was at a drama group for my daughter with my six-month-old son. I didn't have a potty, and I couldn't leave my daughter alone.

I didn't think it was fair to drag her out, so I hid behind some scenery and held my baby in a squat position with a partially open nappy. The air was enough for him to do his business into his nappy and I discreetly changed him.

Feeling guilty about missing a wee or poo

Unfortunately this feeling is all too common. One minute, parents are recognising their baby's communication and catching most of his waste. Then, suddenly, there is a wee or poo in his nappy, and the mum has no idea when it got there. She feels bad that she didn't recognise his signal. The truth is that he probably didn't let her know about it. Babies are not always consistent with their communication. Perhaps he was thinking about something else. Or it might be that his poo felt different today. This often happens during illness. Don't feel guilty about it!

As I mentioned above, parents are sometimes in the situation where they *do* know that their baby is communicating a need to go, but for some reason they are unable to offer them the chance. This didn't happen very much with my first baby, but when it did, I felt guilty. But when I had my second child, I often had to make compromises, and I regularly had to ignore full-bladder signals from my son. When I first heard him cry, I thought it meant: 'Mummy – take me to the potty!' He may even have looked at me to see if I would; when I couldn't, I felt I was letting him down. Then I realised that, before 12 months, it's much more likely that the cry means, 'I have an uncomfortable feeling in my tummy!' And it *is* uncomfortable, but it's not *painful*. Your baby won't feel betrayed or ashamed if you let him wet his nappy – babies are not capable of having such complex thoughts at this age. He will feel happy enough the moment he goes. Of course, if that happens often, then you might start to lose some of the good work you have done building up associations, and he may signal less often. But that doesn't make you a bad parent!

'With my first child I sometimes felt guilty and frustrated that I couldn't read her signals 100 per cent – I was really missing the cultural understanding of how the method works in real life. With my second child, I knew what to expect – I was much more able to relax and follow his lead. Stuff feeling guilty! No need.'

Antonia, mum to Miffy, seven years, and Steffan, three years

Summary

- You can use a variety of places including: a potty, the toilet, the sink and the bushes.
- You don't have to offer the potty when you are out and about, but with a little forethought it can be simple and rewarding.
- Try to take other people's feelings into account when you potty your baby, especially if you are in their house.
- If you know he needs to go but can't get to a potty, you can talk to him and perhaps help him wee into his nappy.
- There's no need to feel guilty about misses.

Chapter 7

BLPT at Night

Whether or not you do BLPT, you can't change the fact that your baby will need to wee in the night, and will almost certainly rouse himself in order to do so. In the first few months he'll usually wee and feed each time he wakes. As he gets older, he'll wee less often, even if he is still waking for milk. But it's important to stress that *you don't have to offer a potty at night*. I take a very pragmatic view towards nights – do whatever you need to do to get more sleep!

Offering the potty at night

When my first child was a baby, she was very sensitive to a full bladder and would not latch on for a feed if she needed to go. This was also the case at night. So I found that if I didn't potty her at night, then she would fidget around, popping on and off the breast. If I persisted to ignore her signals then, after a minute or two of wriggling, and occasionally a bit of crying, she would wee in her nappy and then latch on for a feed. However, I found that if I picked her up and put her on the potty at the first wriggle, then she would wee immediately. She would then be completely relaxed for her feed and would drop back to sleep very quickly. In general, I found that everyone got back to sleep quicker if I offered the potty at night. I became rather adept at doing it – I could do it with minimal fuss with only the light of the nightlight.

One of the things I liked about pottying at night was the fact that it seemed to go a lot more smoothly than during the day. There were no other distractions for me or my baby, and it was very predictable. When she was older and occasionally resisting the potty, I found nights worked well. Because she was drowsy, there was less interference from her conscious mind and her conditioned response was stronger. I would wake up to find my baby wriggling around, and I would offer the potty. She would wee and then feed back to sleep.

My daughter's night-time signals indicating a need to wee included wriggling, heavy breathing, lying on her front with her bottom in the air (to take the weight off her bladder) or occasionally a sharp cry. I found that she would only tend to vocalise if I left it longer than usual – for example if I was in a deep sleep, or if I was downstairs and hadn't picked up on her wriggling through the monitor.

Be prepared

If you are thinking of pottying at night, then I think it's really useful to have everything you need at the side of the bed or cot. I'd suggest having the potty, nappies and whatever you use to wipe, all in arm's reach. A Victorian-style child's chamber pot, with its bulb-shaped bowl and sturdy handle (see page 95) is perfect for night-time as it fits very securely between crossed legs and it is virtually non-spill, even when knocked over. One mum I know told me that she always took her baby to the loo in the night – lights on and everything. Maybe she even flushed. Personally, I am too lazy to leave the bed at night, let alone the room, so I liked to have everything on hand.

You can guard against spillage by putting something absorbent in the potty – some loo roll, a muslin or a cloth nappy. If I'm honest, I did find it tiring having to sit up in bed to offer the potty. However, it was more tiring having to resettle an uncomfortable baby.

Does it matter where your baby sleeps?

I don't think where a baby sleeps makes that much difference to whether or not his parents can offer the potty at night. I found that I could pick up on my daughter's signals whether she was lying next to me or whether she was in a different room, especially if we were using a monitor. However, I could certainly pick up on signals much *sooner* if we were lying next to each other.

If your baby is in a separate room, and it takes longer to respond, then there is a danger he may wake himself up properly and have difficulty getting back to sleep. But this is exactly the same issue that parents already face with night feeding. So, however you choose to do it, you can approach night pottying in the same way.

Sleep has always been my priority, so once I had turned in for the night, I preferred to have my baby on hand.

> *'Co-sleeping and baby wearing seem to make BLPT much easier as babies don't seem to wee when they are snuggled up next to someone (or they give very obvious cues).'*
> **Alastair and Michelle, parents to Iris, four years, and Gabriel, six months**

Simultaneous pottying and feeding

Some babies like to wee and feed at the same time – this is possible if you are willing to give it a try, but takes a bit of practice to get right. It's probably best to practise it in the daytime first. You'll find a description and picture of this position back in Chapter 4. If you aren't keen on feeding your baby while pottying in the night, you may be able to get away with just giving your baby something to suck, for example your finger or a dummy, if you use one.

Resistance to the potty

My son, unlike my daughter, usually objected to me taking him to the potty in the night. He just wanted to feed and sleep. I think he was quite happy to wee during a feed, and it certainly didn't seem to stop him going back to sleep. With both my children I was happy to be led by their individual preferences at night. The fact that I didn't have to sit up in bed to put my son on the potty felt like an advantage.

Although I didn't generally potty him at night, I didn't rule it out either. Sometimes in the early months he would seem uncomfortable in the night and wouldn't settle for a feed – in that case I would try him on the pot and he would often produce something. At around four months of age he went through a phase of pooing in the early hours of the morning, perhaps 4 or 5am. During that time he was very co-operative about going on the potty. If I hadn't pottied him I expect he would have fussed and grunted for a number of minutes, disturbing everyone, until he pooed in his nappy, which I then would have had to change, so it seemed rather better to help him on the potty! From around five months I stopped offering him the potty at night completely, as he got very upset at the suggestion.

Not offering the potty at night

If you don't want to use the potty during the night, your baby will soon come to understand that you don't offer it when the lights are out, and he can wee in his nappy instead. Like all babies, he may still wake to wee, but he won't expect to use the potty.

> *'Sometimes there is a lot of grunting at 4am so we have tried to toilet him then, with mixed success. Otherwise I don't have the energy to do EC at night.'*
>
> **Leila, mum to Sam, five months**

The best nappies for night

There are many different options for night-time nappies. If you are pottying at night, the tricky part is finding the balance between ease of pottying and less disturbance for the baby on the one hand, and guarding against a wet bed on the other. Ultimately, the priority should be more sleep for you and your baby. You don't want your baby crying from being undressed in the night, nor do you want to be changing the sheets.

Some parents have their baby sleep naked on a pile of prefold nappies on a sheepskin or other waterproof layer. The thinking goes that if their baby misses in the night, the parent can pull out the wet prefold without fuss, and the sheepskin will stop leakage going through to the mattress. Some parents even drape a prefold over the top of their baby to prevent upwards wee. I must say this technique didn't work for me. Either my daughter moved around too much and wet the bed or I was so hyper-alert to every wriggle I couldn't sleep properly.

The next option is a small, easy-to-remove cloth nappy which will absorb one miss, but will start leaking with any more than that. This was best for me and my daughter. It meant that I had to change her after a miss, but I generally found I woke up whenever she needed to go – whether that was in advance and I could help her on the potty, or just after she had been in her nappy.

When I was feeling really tired, I used a disposable nappy. I did still offer the potty at times, but I found that this made it quite difficult for me to keep awareness; it was quite hard to tell whether or not the nappy was wet, which meant sometimes I would find myself holding her on the potty when she had already been in her nappy. The good thing about a disposable was that it meant I could replace it without changing it after a potty trip, or I could leave it on if I knew we had missed.

As my son didn't want to potty at night, I couldn't use cloth nappies with him at night (which would have been my preferred choice), as they leaked and occasionally caused him nappy rash. Instead I opted for a disposable at night. It's possible that I didn't find the perfect type of cloth nappy: I know plenty of other parents who successfully used cloth at night without BLPT.

There are likely to be many different solutions, which will change according to how you are feeling, and your baby's stage of development.

Bed protection

Whether or not you decide to potty at night, but especially if you do, it is vital to protect the bed against misses and leaks. This should be the cot and the big bed, or wherever your baby sleeps – even if he's only there for part of the night.

I think that the best solution is a waterproof mattress cover which extends the full width and length of the bed or cot (yes, even the super-king if you are lucky enough to have one!) because it will be Sod's law that your baby will manage to squirm his way over to the unprotected section and wee there. Waterproof covers can make the bed feel hot and sweaty, so it's always best to go for a breathable one. Cheap ones lose their waterproofing after not many washes, so can be false economy.

Another option is to use a very thick Witney (or similar) wool blanket under the sheet. I managed to find one big enough in a charity shop. These blankets have some waterproofing qualities and are very breathable. Hot washing will help to felt them and reduce the chance of wee soaking through. It's always a good idea to have some towels or big flat nappies on hand to spread over any misses; then you can deal with the sheets in the morning.

A lesson can be learned from my friend Annie: she wasn't too careful with her first child, so now the mattress cover is to protect the family from the mattress rather than the other way around!

Cycles of weeing, feeding and waking

A common question is whether night-time pottying affects your baby's ability to sleep through the night. From my experience of my two children, one of whom pottied at night and one of whom did not, it didn't make any difference to how much they woke at night. However, many parents worry that their baby will wake himself for a wee but then need a feed to go back to sleep, and so continuing the cycle of wake, wee, feed, wake, wee, feed ... and so on. I certainly agonised about this too. I had been told to expect my daughter to start sleeping through from around 12 weeks, so when she didn't I started looking for reasons.

I closely observed my baby's behaviour and I found that in the first six months, pretty much every time she woke, she needed a wee and a feed. Then from around six months she didn't always need both. It became a little more complicated to know what to do when she woke; I had to pay close attention to her signals. I found that if she was breathing heavily, kicking her legs or sticking her bottom up, then she wanted a wee, and if she was turning her head from side to side without the other signs, then she may just want a feed. Sometimes, if I offered her a wee at one of those times, she would protest and back-arch, clearly telling me 'no'. Sometimes she would go without weeing for up to eight hours at night. I found that by 12 months my daughter was still feeding two or three times in the night but she would regularly hold her bladder for 10 or more hours.

Many families practising BLPT report similar experiences. This suggests to me that the relationship between feeding and weeing is not as direct as one might expect. We know that there are other factors at play during sleep. Even little babies tend not to wee during a deep sleep. As a baby grows older, he produces a hormone called vasopressin when he sleeps; this acts on the kidneys to make them concentrate urine. Less urine is produced, but it is stronger in both colour and smell. (For more on the role of vasopressin and sleep, see page 222.)

'Pre-emptive' or 'dream wees'

Some parents employ a specific tactic to help guard against the cycle of wake, wee, feed. Jenn Conn, who founded the www.bornready.uk website and forum, is a big fan of what she calls the 'pre-emptive wee', or 'dream wee'. What happens is this: your baby is put to bed and is sleeping deeply. At some point in the evening, you go in to the baby and lift him out of bed. You gently remove his nappy (if he is wearing one) and cue him over a potty. Your baby wees, the nappy is replaced and he is put back to sleep. He never properly wakes up, and so doesn't need to feed back to sleep – thus breaking the cycle. That's the theory anyway! She has recorded a wonderful video demonstration which is available to watch on YouTube.[1]

Jenn swears by this technique and has successfully used it with all four of her children. I tried this with baby number one and I found it worked very well for a period, although I personally don't think it had much effect on the 'cycle' as my daughter still woke up for a feed.

This process is actually similar to the 'dream *feed*' that some experts recommend[2] – where you give your baby a feed at a convenient time for you but while he isn't fully awake, in the hope that he'll sleep for longer.

Whether or not you opt for a dream *feed* or a dream *wee* rather depends on whether you believe that your baby is primarily waking up out of hunger or out of a need to wee. Eventually I came to the conclusion that my babies were waking up as a result of sleep cycles, and there wasn't a whole lot that I was prepared to do about it!

However, I did find it useful to potty my daughter at the time I went to bed in the hope that she wouldn't then wake me for a wee 20 minutes later. It takes some balls to do this, even when you have some experience. It can seem rather counter-intuitive to risk disturbing a sleeping baby, especially if you've already spent an hour or more getting your baby to bed in the first place.

Summary

- BLPT at night is optional.
- If your baby is very sensitive to a full bladder, or is passing a bowel movement in the night, then BLPT can help you get more sleep.
- Use a nappy or backup system which strikes a balance between easy access and protection against misses.

- Waterproof the bed to guard against misses and leaks.
- The need to wee at night isn't directly related to the amount of milk drunk.
- Offering your baby a pre-emptive wee may help him (and you) sleep for longer.

Chapter 8

Special Cases

Some families who practise or want to practise BLPT face extra challenges. In any family there are times when life gets a bit too much, and BLPT may need to slip into the background while parents focus their attention elsewhere. However, there are also times when focusing on BLPT actually helps parents concentrate on the things which matter to them most – such as communicating with their babies. Sometimes I hear people say – 'of course, you can't do that with twins', or, 'you can't do that when you have older children', or they rule it out for some other reason. But this kind of attitude stems from the idea that BLPT is an optional extra that you can only do if you have plenty of time on your hands (i.e. you are on maternity leave with your first child) and you want to 'go the extra mile'.

In my view BLPT is not so much an optional extra, but a useful skill that *any* parent should have in their toolkit. If offering a potty can soothe a crying child (which it sometimes can when that baby is troubled by wind or constipation), then parents of twins or large families will find it just as useful as the parent of an only child. Likewise, if BLPT enhances the communication and bond between a parent and baby, then if that baby has autism, the rewards of the method may be even more important.

Twins and multiples

In societies where BLPT is the norm, twins are held out right from the earliest days, just like their singleton peers. In the West, however, people tend to think that having multiples makes BLPT impossible. It is true, of course, that if a baby has a twin (or indeed older siblings), parents can't always give him 100 per cent of their attention. So parents may find it more difficult to notice all of their baby's signals, and also more difficult at times to act on them. But babies and parents *can* still benefit from BLPT in just the same way that singleton families will.

A mother of twin boys in one of my workshops told me that she found BLPT made life easier, precisely *because* she had twins.

> Corinne found that conventional nappy changes were one of the most difficult times in day-to-day life with her twins. Corinne's attention always had to be split between her two sons. She found it much easier to deal with nappy changes in conjunction with offering the potty. Although at times she still had to deal with sudden unexpected sprays of urine and both twins trying to play with the contents of the nappy – these times were much reduced if they were given a chance to use the potty as well. She found it much easier to attend to her second baby if she was supporting her first on the potty, rather than trying to change him too. She felt that, although BLPT is more difficult with twins, 'the benefits also apply twice over'.

Because twins are often born early, and may be smaller than their peers, they may reach physical milestones later. They may need to be held in-arms, or supported on the potty for longer. Corinne's babies were about eight or nine months when they were able to sit on the potty unaided. This made life considerably easier for her, as she could then potty them both at the same time. Simultaneous nappy changes, on the other hand, were still impossible.

Tips for twins

There are a number of practical measures you can take to make life easier when working with twins or multiples:

- **Dress for success:** This applies when you have one child, but is even more important with twins. Dress your babies in easy-access clothes. Have potties, wipes and nappy paraphernalia to hand. Plan in advance how and when you will offer the potty.
- **Make use of other pairs of hands:** If you really want to try BLPT but are finding it overwhelming, then make use of times when your partner is around, or enlist the help of Grandma. The most efficient use of time is to try offering the potty in the first hour of the morning, as this is normally the time that babies wee most often. So if you can only manage to try BLPT for an hour or so at the weekend, then make it first thing.
- **Rely on timing:** More than one child makes it difficult to act spontaneously. So it makes sense to work more with timing, rather than trying to follow your babies' signals. Offer the potty at regular intervals to try to pre-empt their need to go. Commit to offering the potty when your babies wake from their nap, and plan how you can manage this.
- **Use two potties:** Make sure you have one potty for each child. They are unlikely to wait patiently, and it saves time if you can potty them simultaneously.
- **Remember that twins are individuals:** Your babies may well be interested in different things and they will learn in different ways. You may find that one baby catches on faster than the other. Don't worry, they'll both get there in the end.
- **Have realistic expectations:** Raising twins will be hard work and there will be a steep learning curve. Don't set yourself unrealistic targets. I know some parents who were hoping to raise their twins 100 per cent nappy free from birth. This is an extremely difficult task in our society and climate, even with one child. Once their twins were born, these parents felt overwhelmed by the task and lost confidence in the

method. Understand that you will have lots of misses – they are an integral part of the process. If you set your sights too high, you may feel disheartened and fail to see the benefits you are achieving.

Physical complications

Sometimes a baby may have some extra physical complication that makes normal handling difficult, and parents may feel that BLPT won't be possible. Physical complications don't necessarily rule out BLPT, however. All babies need to have their waste managed for them in some form or other, and BLPT may bring specific advantages. I have heard some impressive stories of how parents have managed to adapt to particular challenges, and have still been able to reap the benefits of the method.

In the below example, Cathy's daughter was diagnosed with developmental hip dysplasia shortly after birth. This is a fairly common condition that occurs in about 1 in 1,000 babies in the UK, where the femur is out of alignment with the pelvis. In order to establish correct positioning and normal growth, the baby's hips need to be held in an open position, with the knees bent (mimicking the natural position for mothers to carry their babies). In order to replicate this position, doctors recommend full-time use of a Pavlik harness for around three months.

> Cathy had used BLPT techniques with her first child, and so was keen to see the same benefits when her second daughter was born. Undeterred by the hip dysplasia diagnosis and harness, Cathy continued to offer her baby the potty. She found that the harness sometimes made things slightly easier, as it helped to support her baby in the 'squat' position. Although she had a spare harness, she was keen to prevent it from being soiled, which was an occasional risk when offering the potty. On

balance, however, she felt that it was just as likely to be soiled by a loose stool if she had been using nappies conventionally. Cathy managed to continue offering the potty throughout the three months that her baby wore the harness, at which point the condition was completely rectified.

In some circumstances, parents may even find that BLPT helps with the physical complications, as the extra awareness the method brings to bodily processes can be of special benefit. BLPT encourages parents to be fully present with their babies when they are passing waste, and this can make all the difference when this act is a struggle.

In the example below, Angie's son was born with an ano-rectal malformation called Hirschsprung's disease, where nerves are absent from the large intestine. Her son had to have an operation to improve the function of his bowel, and he needs to have regular washouts, to keep him from getting constipated. Her son's condition would probably have meant that Angie would have been attuned to his movements even if she did not know about BLPT. However, her previous experience and knowledge of the method with her older children enabled her to approach the situation with far more confidence. Angie describes how using the principles of BLPT has significantly helped the family manage his condition:

'We are thrilled at how listening to his body has helped with his experience. We don't yet hold him out – as, until very recently, he hated to be away from our bodies. I guess we don't do EC by strict standards, but it's way more than I thought or was led to believe was possible. We had three doctors looking at our totally natural nappy cream in amazement because they couldn't believe he didn't have nappy rash. We did have one incident where my poorly husband was looking after him and missed a poo, so he was unchanged for about 45 minutes, and he did get an awful, blistering rash, so we know that he does have the very acidic Hirschsprung's poo – and *it is the combination of frequent changes and gentle nappy cream that is generally keeping him rash-free.'*

Angie, mum to Freddy, six months

Special needs

I have been asked whether it is possible for children with special needs to practise BLPT. I have not worked extensively with children with special needs, and, even if I had, individual needs vary so much, across such a broad spectrum of conditions, that it would be impossible to give any kind of 'one size fits all' answer.

However, I have heard some truly inspirational accounts of parents of children with special needs who have tried BLPT. What struck me from these stories is how empowering the parents found the process. Even if they did not achieve the same level of 'catch rate' that they might have hoped for, or if BLPT did not result in early toilet independence, these parents were still grateful for the opportunity to communicate with their babies in this extra way. And in many cases, the abilities of their babies far surpassed anything they would have expected.

Vicky's son was diagnosed with autism when he was 14 months old. Despite his condition, she was able to practise BLPT to typical levels throughout much of his babyhood. Vicky explains how the method itself helped her to bond with her baby, even though communication was sometimes difficult:

'Even though at a young age, we knew there was something different with my son, BLPT definitely helped in communication. I felt I knew my baby better – it was like there was more trust from him to me, and it all clicked together with how he was feeling – just a closer, better bond. He had potty strike at about 11 months, due to his autism, and we then went back to part-time BLPT in the house only, and he fully regressed around 13–14 months. He's three next week and he's still in nappies. He knows you go to the toilet

for pees, but he just chooses not to. My advice to other parents with babies with autism is to really keep everything baby-led, and to not push anything. The only thing I do now is let him run around half naked with potty sitting. If he goes and sits on it, I'll say "pee pee, pss pss" but we're still waiting to see.'

Vicky, mum to Jack, almost three years

Working with delay

Momma Jorje is a parenting blogger in the US who writes on www.mommajorje.com, and she is an expert on BLPT. Her third child, a son, was diagnosed with Down's syndrome while she was pregnant.

'I wondered if anyone with a child with Down's syndrome had ever used elimination communication … I'm not sure why I was worried – as if there would be some reason why I shouldn't do it! When Spencer was five weeks old, I noticed him start to fuss a little. Instead of going straight for the breast, I found his nappy was dry and thought he might be fussing with a need to pee. I stripped his nappy off, cradled him over a bowl and cued him. He peed immediately! It was my first try!'

Momma Jorje, mum to Spencer, three years

Momma Jorje points out that she was very lucky that her son Spencer had no muscle-tone issues, as this is a common characteristic of Down's syndrome. 'I could see how a baby with low muscle tone might be more difficult to hold over a potty,' she says. 'I think once a parent gets the hang of holding their newborn, though, they could then figure out how best to hold their baby over a receptacle.' It seems to me that the in-arms potty position is likely to be useful for a longer period. The fact that your baby may reach significant milestones later than his peers is not a problem for the purposes of BLPT. In fact, it may make things easier. Babies tend to be more co-operative during the in-arms phase – so if this lasts longer, then that's an advantage for BLPT!

'I started EC when my little girl was 10 months. She has responded brilliantly. In less than a month all her solids were on the potty. We just take her as she wakes up, after naps, and before her bath. My only regret is I let the Down's syndrome diagnosis make me "give up" the idea of ECing until she was 10 months old.'

Tia, mum to Georgia, 12 months

Conventional potty training may not be appropriate

In Chapter 15 I will discuss how conventional potty training relates to BLPT. One aspect is relevant here, however. The standard advice for all children, often including those with special needs, is to wait until they can follow spoken instructions. If your child has a developmental delay, this milestone may occur later. Waiting until he can understand spoken instructions could mean that your child wears nappies for longer than necessary.

> Rachel did not set out to do BLPT with her son who has Down's syndrome, but when he turned one she found she could predict when he might poo – usually after meals. It made a lot of sense to her to sit him on the potty at those times. He was very happy to stay on the potty while he watched his big brother or played with his toys – being less mobile probably helped. It wasn't long before he cottoned on to the idea. In this way he stopped soiling his nappies many months – even years – before some of his peers. It took more time and a lot of praise and encouragement to teach him to use the potty for wees too.

The charity PromoCon, which exists to provide support for families affected by continence issues and to spread understanding and awareness, is critical of the 'wait till they are ready' approach. In its leaflet, 'Information Sheet on Toilet Training Children with Special Needs',[1] PromoCon explains that toilet training relies on two factors: the bodily 'maturation of the bladder and bowel' and the mental development of 'social and cultural awareness'. Children with learning difficulties often have a delay in their toilet training, but this is usually due to a 'lack of understanding and social awareness ... rather than an inherent problem within the bladder or bowel'. Although PromoCon are working on the assumption that potty training should not be 'started until it can be finished', they point out that parents need not wait until their child displays the *social* signs of readiness, commonly thought of as essential to potty training. PromoCon advises: 'rather than waiting for the child ... to be socially aware and motivated before toilet training commences we use maturation of the bladder and bowel as the trigger factor for starting training.'

My belief is that there are many benefits to be gleaned by starting earlier. I think it is possible that by training through conditioning at a younger age, parents may help their babies bypass the need to make an intellectual leap of understanding during toddlerhood. I would love to see more research done in this area.

> *'Spencer also has delays, especially with communication. He's now almost three and he goes through phases where he will actually sign that he needs to potty. Otherwise, I just have to watch timing, watch for his signs and check him. He has this funny tendency to pee just a little so that I will notice he needs to go. I tell people that we transitioned out of diapers (and into training underwear) at 12 months, but that doesn't mean that he was fully "potty trained" or anywhere near potty independent.'*
>
> **Momma Jorje, mum to Spencer, three years**

Focus on communication and meeting needs as they occur

It may be that your baby's specific circumstances mean that BLPT does not translate into zero soiled nappies or a baby potty trained by 18 months. (In fact, it probably won't translate in this way for a typical baby, either!) However, Momma Jorje states that she 'can not think of a single thing that would entirely rule out BLPT for any child with or without Down's syndrome'. I think that the essence of BLPT can be used by *any family*. BLPT is first and foremost about learning about your own baby's needs and behaviours. Parents then learn how to respond to those needs. That may be working with a baby's reflexes to help keep him cleaner, or it may be simply communicating about bodily functions, and changing misses as they occur.

Summary

- You need to consider your own family's unique needs to decide if BLPT is right for you.
- BLPT is not just an 'optional extra' for parents with simple circumstances, but should be seen as part of a toolkit for *any* parent to use.
- Although exceptional circumstances can present challenges to practising BLPT, the method may also bring special benefits as well.

Chapter 9

The Importance of Community

Nowadays there is an abundance of choice: how we dress, how we eat, where we live, what career we pursue, how we spend our leisure time and how we raise our children. While this freedom can allow us to make thoughtful, enlightened decisions about our lifestyle, making decisions can also be stressful. It can be even harder when the decisions you make go against the grain of popular culture. And here I am contributing to this issue by offering parents yet another choice in baby care. Most people in the Western world don't offer the potty in the first year. In time, this will change, as more parents learn about the benefits and ease of the method. But, until then, you will probably encounter many people who nappied and potty trained differently to you. It may be that those closest to you – your mum, your best friend, your NCT group – did, or are doing, things differently.

Arguing your case with friends and family

Some people can find it difficult to accept that you are doing things differently. They may feel that your different choice implies some kind of criticism of them. They may feel defensive about their own choices, and this may manifest itself in a criticism of *yours*. It's tempting to argue your case, but that is unlikely to help. The more you defend yourself, the more they feel attacked, and so on in a vicious circle. It helps if you can recognise that their defensiveness comes from their own feelings of insecurity. They may feel that they didn't or don't have the same kind of freedom, support, knowledge or ability to make the choices that you have made.

It's also worth asking yourself: how do *you* feel about the subject? Are *you* defensive about it? I know I was at first. As the months and years went by, I've found myself getting a lot more relaxed: it doesn't bother me what anyone else thinks. I still want to promote the practice, but I don't judge people who choose differently.

Defensiveness leads to unhelpful ways of talking with each other. It may be best to avoid the subject. However, if this is impossible, you can explain how a person's attitude is making you feel unsupported and hurt (if it is). This may be enough for them to re-evaluate their way of speaking to you. Once there is genuine dialogue between you, and you are both trying to listen to each other and meet each other's needs, then they may come to understand the benefits. Sometimes it can be best to just shrug and smile.

Convincing partners

The BLPT approach is not just for mums. I know many dads who are extremely dedicated to the method – some more so than their partners. However, in the main, mothers get to know their baby more quickly during the first few weeks. Mums can work out which cry means what, and she may be better able to keep track of a baby's routine needs. This can mean that she is better able to predict potty calls. Dads can feel left out and disempowered. Of course, that could be true for either partner.

If your partner is hesitant about BLPT, watching it in action could be a great way to win them over. If possible, demonstrate how it works, and hopefully the results will speak for themselves. Sceptics may become believers and proud of their little baby's achievements. Even better is if your *partner* takes your baby to the potty. It's really important that you are almost *certain* that your baby will go; if he doesn't produce anything, your partner may feel they have embarrassed themselves trying for nothing. However, if they try it and get a catch – they may be won over.

If someone is truly set against trying, then it's unlikely that reasoned arguments will convince them. You may find it easier to focus on it in their absence, especially during the learning period – in time they may come round, especially once they see it working well. Babies can easily adapt to the idea that one parent offers them the potty, while another does not. (I'll discuss this more in the next chapter, in relation to childcare.)

Just another word about dads – one of the things I love is that dads can do BLPT *just as well as mums*. It's a really lovely way for dads to bond with their baby and gain more confidence. So if you think your partner can be brought round, it's really worth persevering: the pay-off can be immeasurable.

> *'BLPT seems to be one part of early parenting which the dad can help out with – it gave me a great opportunity for bonding with my babies.'*
>
> **Alastair, dad to Iris, four years,**
> **and Gabriel, six months**

Coping with criticism

Sometimes strangers or acquaintances make comments about the way you raise your child. Only last week on a cold day I was cycling with my son in a bike seat. As I pulled up at some traffic lights, a pedestrian called out, 'He looks absolutely freezing!' As he was well dressed in a thick coat and hat, I felt fairly confident he was okay. However, a less confident mother might have felt attacked and undermined. (In fact, I just smiled and cycled on.) I'm sure these comments are well meaning, but they can really knock your confidence, especially in the vulnerable first few weeks, when everything is new.

'The first time around, I got a lot of negative criticism. People didn't know about BLPT then (my eldest is over nine years old now) and so people thought I was "forcing" him to "potty train" and they assumed that all I did with him all day was sit him on a potty – they thought that was cruel because they figured it never gave him a chance to play. They couldn't have been further from the truth, but, as a first-time mum, any criticism can be hard.

I didn't do anything differently with the next baby, but I had that much more confidence in myself, and because of more information and news about it (through documentaries and newspaper stories, etc.), more people knew a bit about it – I don't ever remember receiving criticism about it second time around. I got a lot of "wow!"s from people, and that was rather refreshing and positive!'

**Shyann, mum to Duncan, nine years,
and Hamish, four and a half years**

In the main, criticisms like these stem from ignorance. It's helpful to remember that advice on baby care *does* change quickly. In the not-so-distant past, mothers were told to put babies to sleep on their fronts, not their backs, and babies began solids sometimes as early as two or three months. Although it's not an excuse for unwanted advice, we can't expect everyone to keep up to date. It may not be so long ago that *you* thought early potty training was impossible! Also, we have a tendency to think the latest advice is the best. The case of nappies and potty training, however, teaches us to be a bit more sceptical about that – some of the older ways were better!

Comments can also come from another type of ignorance – an ignorance of your particular circumstances. For all that passer-by knew, I could have been feeling really terrible that my son was cold on the bike. Perhaps I had asked him 20 times to put on his gloves, or I had to rush to do the school pick-up, or I couldn't afford a car – or any number of reasons why I might have had to let him be cold.

It's not always easy to deflect unwanted criticism. However, feeling confident about your choices helps, and you can cultivate confidence by seeking out support.

Finding support

Perhaps the parents around you are accepting about your choice to do things a little differently. That's really helpful, but if you don't actually know any other parents who are doing BLPT, then you miss out on a lot of support. Raising a baby is a time for learning, and it's completely natural to ask for support and advice.

In countries where early potty training is the norm, mothers can ask any woman for advice; everyone understands the merits of helping their baby to void in an appropriate place. Also, mothers are simply expected to start potty training from birth, so there is no conscious decision to be made – they aren't going against convention. This makes practising the method so much easier – especially in the early days.

As I said in Chapter 5, it is *doubt* that creates the biggest hurdle to getting started. It's *doubt* that can make you hesitate to try your baby on the potty. It's *doubt* that can make you feel silly when you hold your baby out for the first time. Having an entire community that expects you to potty train early, and supports you as you do it, eliminates this sense of doubt.

> *'My whole family potty her, and they have been really supportive, which has made the process a lot easier, and it meant there was no confusion for her.'*
>
> **Mel, mum to Emma, 20 months**

Helpful talk

Often, other people won't have a specific answer to your problem, but the real-time support they offer can help you work out your own answer.

In order to provide you with the right kind of support, they need to have an understanding of what BLPT is all about, and why you want to do it; ideally, they've been there themselves. For example, let's say you can't seem to get the first catches and establish the connection. A conversation with your friend might go something like this:

You: 'I keep thinking he wants to wee, but by the time I get his nappy off, he's already gone – it's really frustrating.'
Inexperienced friend: 'Oh, dear. It sounds like a lot of work. There's no way I could tell when my baby was about to wee. Perhaps you are making things too hard for yourself.'

Your friend means well, but she's not able to support you in your choice. On the other hand, a friend who understands why you want to try BLPT might say something different:

Experienced friend: 'That can be disheartening at first. Hang in there and keep trying, because you'll get a catch sooner or later. Why don't you try dressing him in just a T-shirt and socks for a while, and see if that makes things easier?'

If you can, it's really helpful to surround yourself with more people who talk like this!

Seeking a local community

Once you have accepted that you need a supportive BLPT community, you can start looking for it. It won't be hard to find in some form or other. The very best kind of community is real-life friends that you hang out with in your home town. You can start with your friends and acquaintances – especially those with babies the same age, or who are expecting. Mention that you've heard of BLPT and are trying it out. You may find that some of them are also doing it – if so, perfect: you have a ready-made community! If they are new to the idea, and seem interested, you can give them some more information and point them to a website or lend them this book. Tread carefully: you don't want them to think you are criticising them. In fact, new mothers are often very open to experimentation, so this may not be as hard as it seems. If you have friends who are practising BLPT, or considering trying it out, then you can encourage each other. You can organise play dates when you can have the potties out and share tips and equipment.

If no one in your current network is interested in BLPT, you can try finding local like-minded people. There are probably already people in your area who are practising it. The chances are that they are also looking for support. Groups such as NCT, Sling Meet, Sing and Sign, La Leche League and Baby Café are great places to meet people (for more on these, see the Resources section, page 239). Mention to the leaders that you are looking for others practising BLPT, and ask them to pass on your details.

Children's centres are another good place. Sometimes they run mother-and-baby groups, specifically for mothers to meet each other. I've sometimes come into these groups as a guest speaker, and I normally find that two or three of the parents are already practising BLPT – often without realising the others are! Again, you can tell staff that you are looking for other families doing it, or even put up a little poster on the notice board.

My experience of community

When I started offering my baby the potty in 2008, I did not know a single soul who was also doing it. The benefits I discovered meant I was committed to the method, but I still found it really hard. Misses often knocked my confidence and I felt defensive about it. By chance, I met another mum called Antonia at a La Leche League meeting when my baby was three months and hers, nine months. We struck up a friendship that continues to this day.

By the time I had my second baby, I literally knew over a hundred local families who used the method. What a difference it made! Most of my close friends did it to some degree. It seemed to me that everyone in Oxford had heard of BLPT. I know three families *on my street* who have done it. If I needed support or advice, or I just wanted to share my experience, then I could do that whenever I wanted – on a daily basis if necessary. No one was fazed when I whipped out the potty for my newborn. I was unconcerned about misses. I realised I didn't have anything to prove.

Online support

Of course your greatest resource is likely to be the Internet. You can find out about local groups in your area. Many real-life communities and groups have Yahoo groups or Facebook pages to support them. You can get to know people online and find out about real-life social events in your area. Because it's so practical, BLPT appeals to all sorts of families – not just hippie ones! But parenting groups that focus on other progressive aspects of child rearing, such as breastfeeding, baby-led weaning, slings and attachment parenting, are often good starting points for finding parents who are using BLPT or who want to try it out.

There are also forums and groups specifically dedicated to discussing BLPT. These often go by the American name 'elimination communication' (or 'EC'). Many local BLPT support groups have their own Facebook pages, and, at the time of going to print, there is an active national Facebook page, EC UK. This Facebook page, plus my own website, www.nappyfreebaby.co.uk, publishes details of local BLPT support groups. These are also good places to advertise if you are interested in meeting other parents practising BLPT in your area. Most of the major baby information websites, such as Mumsnet and BabyCenter, have forum threads dedicated to the subject. Because babies grow up so fast, these groups tend to come and go, as the interests of the parents turn to other things; however, these forums often have a wealth of information in the archive. The active ones can also provide invaluable real-time support, for when you need a bit of encouragement.

Summary

- The choices available to parents today can allow us to make enlightened decisions about the way we raise our babies. They can also leave us feeling bewildered and unsupported, especially if we go against the grain of popular culture.
- Parenting is a highly emotive subject, and many parents, especially first-time ones, encounter criticism of their choices.
- Finding a supportive community can help you feel confident. Supportive friends can offer practical advice or just a listening ear.
- Understanding the value of community is the first step to finding it.

Chapter 10

The Impact of Developmental Changes at 6–12 Months

The six-to-twelve-month period is one of phenomenal growth and development for a baby. At the beginning of this period, he is just about able, or almost able, to sit unaided, but by twelve months he will probably be pulling up to standing, crawling, cruising and perhaps even walking. There is enormous change going on in his brain too. A baby will learn to gesture to communicate, and may say his first words. He will start to recognise himself as a separate being. He will have to get to grips with eating solid foods and he will probably cut his first teeth.

In this chapter I'll explore how these factors have an effect on BLPT with your baby. Parents who wish to begin BLPT with a baby of this age will find a step-by-step guide in Chapter 11, 'Getting Started at 6–12 Months'.

Physical developments

It is very common during spells of intense developmental change for babies to resist being handled in certain ways. When my first baby was learning to sit, I found that she hated to be held in the squat position

– she wanted to do it all for herself. We bought a toilet seat insert and this solved the problem as she was very happy to sit on top of it! After a week or so, she was then happy to be held in the potty position again. This seems to be a common theme for babies who are on the cusp of acquiring a major new skill – and there are a lot of new skills to learn during this period!

Gross motor skills

Perhaps the most obvious changes to an onlooker are the advances in gross motor skills that a baby goes through over the next six months. He is likely to go from just (or almost) sitting, to crawling, standing, cruising and walking. Becoming mobile, and therefore being able to independently pursue his own agenda, is a major milestone for a baby. He is increasingly able to make clear what he wants, and before long he may even be able to get to it by himself. Your baby will probably want to spend less time sitting on your lap or in your arms, and will relish being able to move about the room. This may make it harder to spot toilet signals, as your baby is literally further away from you, but it also means that he can begin to take a more active part in the process.

> *'Now that Natasha's getting bigger it's funny to see her interest in the contents of the potty, and she always waves bye-bye to it when it goes to be emptied, which is cute!'*
>
> **Kathryn, mum to Natasha, 10 months**

Your baby might start to show some resistance to pottying at this stage. Although younger babies are typically co-operative and amenable to this, it's the parent who makes the potty trip happen. Most babies under six months are happy to be dangled here, there and anywhere as they do their business. A younger baby will hardly notice if you whisk him off to the potty mid-play; he will be immediately distracted by a mirror or a song, for example. An older baby, however, is a different kettle of fish. As he gets older and more physically competent, he will be able to claim much more ownership of the process. Your baby will almost certainly start to object if you move him about too quickly, or expect him to sit on the potty with nothing to do. It's important not to put your baby off the potty by insisting he sits when he has other ideas. But, on the other hand, don't be afraid to offer. If you begin to hold him out and he protests, then you can simply let him go back to what he was doing. It's not a problem to ask the question, and then listen to your baby's answer of 'no'. (As long as you don't do it too much, that is!)

Standing practice

A baby's muscular control moves in a roughly downwards direction: first he gets head and neck control, next the top, middle and base of the spine, and then through the limbs and into the fingers and toes. Once your baby starts to get strength in his legs, he may seem to want to practise standing *all* the time. You might find he is too occupied with this to allow you to potty him: when you try to hold him in the squat position, he may simply straighten out like a board. This phase will pass, but, in the meantime, it can feel frustrating. You can try helping your baby wee while standing – the bath, shower or outdoors may be the best place. However, you may find that the effort involved in standing makes it hard for him to release. You can try to distract him long enough to help him do a wee before the standing practice begins again. Parents often find outside is the best.

Another possibility is in front of a mirror, where he can see your face. It may also help if you really try to give your baby lots of time for standing, so that he 'has his fill', so to speak, and may be more willing to sit or be held. This may even physically tire him out. Even if that doesn't work, it should help the phase pass more quickly. Once your baby has mastered the skill of standing, he will probably be happy to sit again.

Teething

Children experience teething to different degrees. Some seem to sprout their teeth overnight without so much as a grimace; others are out of sorts for weeks. In our house, teething had a significant effect on BLPT.

Teething pain normally lasts for up to two weeks per tooth, and occurs immediately before a tooth erupts (in the case of molars, before each 'bump' erupts). The characteristics of tooth pain are normally quite clear – and (assuming your baby suffers from teething) you will get to recognise your baby's unique signs of discomfort. Both my children found it very difficult to get to sleep. They would press their jaws against my face or chest, or the mattress. They would sleep fitfully and wake many times in the night. They were generally irritable, clingy and quick to upset during the day. They would occasionally bite. They dribbled at times, and occasionally gnawed in a frenzied fashion. (This was quite distinct from the 'chewing' phase they went through at around four months.)

I found that teething greatly affected my babies' bladder and bowel function. During teething, my daughter was prone to diarrhoea. I was unclear whether the pain caused her system to empty, or whether it was due to the excess of saliva she was swallowing. This sometimes resulted in unexpected misses. She was vulnerable to nappy rash at such times. In both of my children, urination became much more frequent during teething and signals seemed to disappear entirely. They also sometimes resisted the potty. I think that the chronic, and sometimes acute, pain they experienced made it hard for them to recognise bladder discomfort or empty their bladder fully. It may be possible that a decrease in the hormone vasopressin, due to the pain and stress, resulted in a higher volume of urine.

The majority of a baby's teeth are cut between 12 and 24 months. Of their 20 teeth, the front 8 may cause a couple of weeks of disruption each, and the larger teeth could affect them for up to a month each. If they all came through separately, that could mean up to 16 solid months of teething! I think it's important parents recognise what a major influence teething can be, so that they can recalibrate their expectations during episodes.

If your baby is affected by teething, it's very likely that you will see a big change in your 'catch rate' and communication. Don't let this worry you: it's normal, and it will certainly pass. But don't let me scaremonger either: many children only display teething symptoms the day or two immediately before the tooth breaks through. Some don't seem to notice at all.

Mental developments

Of course, physical developments don't happen in isolation, they develop in tandem with the brain. As babies grow they become more interested in the outside world than their internal workings; this can lead them to be less interested in using the potty, or it can result in them being more interested in it! Whichever way it goes, it's normally possible to keep up with the changes and provide the stimulation your baby needs while he is on the potty to stop him getting bored. Placing a little table for his toys in front of the potty is a lovely way to keep him involved.

Introducing solids

When babies are exclusively milk-fed, their stools tend to be runny, 'seedy', yellow or orange in colour and not unpleasant smelling. However, it all changes when they start solid food. In the past, this change in diet, and therefore in poo, often triggered the start of potty training. Mothers were encouraged by three main factors: firstly, the poos themselves become more unpleasant. Washing out solid poo from cloth nappies is a much more difficult task, so mothers were motivated to catch stools if they could. Secondly, babies of this age are more able to sit on a potty by themselves (although in previous decades, weaning was traditionally started much earlier). And, thirdly, babies themselves seem to acquire more bowel control.

Whether or not you use cloth nappies, these factors remain in place; despite what the nappy companies might like to imply, you still have to handle faeces even if you use disposables! This means you will probably find BLPT easier (and be more motivated to keep it up), once your baby is on solids.

Changing poos and wees

At first, especially if families are offering finger foods from the outset, the runny poos are often exactly the same – except with the hilarious addition of, for example, a single whole pea, or sprig of broccoli. But as time goes by, and your baby gets more efficient at chewing, food is better digested and his poos get firmer. Firmer stools can make BLPT easier, as your baby may give clearer signals that he has a full bowel. He may display conscious signals as he himself recognises the sensation – perhaps by looking surprised or uncomfortable, or by tugging his nappy. Even if he doesn't consciously communicate, he is more likely to grunt and go red-faced as he starts to push.

His wees will also change as more solid food is introduced. They change in smell, which means you may want to be more careful to protect against misses. Eventually, as your baby's diet switches from liquid towards solid, wees will also get less frequent.

The frequency of poos may also start to change. Babies who were previously pooing up to 10 times a day may now start producing a regular offering first thing in the morning, or just before bedtime. Not all babies will start passing daily bowel movements; some will continue to poo three or more times a day. Pooing patterns are certainly very personal and particular to each child. However, after discussing the pooing habits of literally hundreds of babies (I love my job!), it seems to me that babies who are offered the potty move more quickly towards a larger daily poo. I suspect that babies who are not actively encouraged to poo (through being provided with an opportunity and a comfortable position) tend not to empty their bowel as fully – leading to more poos a day.

Constipation

It is not unusual for slight constipation to occur at this stage. Firmer stools can be unsettling for some babies. They may try to resist the urge to push. This compounds the problem, as the longer stools stay in the bowel, the harder they become. BLPT can help relieve this problem. An old friend of mine was nappying her baby conventionally, and when she started on solids at six months, she went from her regular daily poo to nothing for three days. The little girl was acting as if she had stomach cramps and her mother wanted to help. She had seen babies using potties lots of times before, so she tried holding her daughter over the loo when she sensed her baby was feeling the urge to push. Sure enough, with a little verbal encouragement, her baby was able to pass her bowel movement. As her baby continued to act uncomfortable and unwilling to poo in her nappy, her mum carried on helping her over the next few days. Very soon, her baby was plainly expressing a preference to being held over the toilet, and she became regular in her pooing habits again.

Some health professionals suggest that early potty training itself is responsible for constipation.[1] However, a 2002 study of 406 children found that earlier toilet training 'is not associated with constipation, stool withholding, or stool toileting refusal'.[2] I think that the tendency towards constipation lies within the child themselves. Of my children, one showed a distinct preference for the potty and also slightly tended towards constipation, while the other seemed less able to control bowel movements and was more regular. If your child has a propensity towards constipation, then it is most likely that this would happen whether or not you practise BLPT.

I've seen many cases where offering a potty eases the situation, as parents offer their baby clear opportunities to go and provide active support during the process. However, once you start doing this, then you need to be aware that your baby may come to rely on that support.

Helping your baby pass a stool

If your baby seems to be struggling to pass a stool, there is a danger that it can make a small tear, which could be distressing for him and potentially make him fear passing a bowel movement. To help your baby defecate, you can gently press his perineum to help the poo ease out of his anus. This can feel awkward; try holding his left leg as normal and using your right wrist to support his right leg, leaving your fingers free to press his perineum.

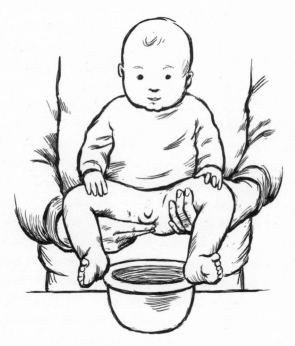

Keeping track of his poos

If your child tends towards constipation, you need to have a sense of what is happening in the bowel so you can take measures if necessary. Scientists have found that just looking at frequency can be misleading.[3] Children who are constipated may defecate daily. I have found it useful to occasionally feed my children something recognisable like kiwi fruit, sweetcorn or blackberries; this can give a rough idea of transit time. In an unconstipated child it will be around 20–40 hours. The most important thing, however, is the type of faeces being passed.

When babies soil their nappies, it can be quite hard to work out what type of stool is being passed. If you are catching poos, however, it's a lot easier to assess them, as they land in the potty relatively intact! Being able to keep tabs on your baby's defecation, and providing assistance or encouragement where necessary, is a useful and important benefit of BLPT.

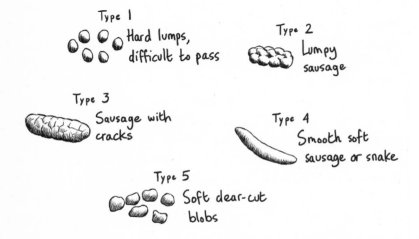

If your baby's poos look like types 1 or 2 in the above illustration, this suggests a longer transit time, and you may need to watch out for constipation. Type 4 is the 'ideal' stool, though a range of 3–5 is normal. Soft stools can be misleading, however, especially if they come unexpectedly: it's possible for a constipated baby (or child or adult) to get 'impacted', which means that dry, hard faeces is causing a blockage, while soft faecal matter slips past. Stools of this kind will not be sausage-shaped and will tend to be sticky. It's also hard to control them, which may lead to more misses.

Of course, not all babies will suffer from constipation. Even when they do, in most babies the matter will resolve itself within a few days.

Taking BLPT to the next level

Many parents start by offering the potty just at change times, or other convenient times. It's perfectly fine to carry on like this at this stage. However, if you would like to see more benefit, you can offer the potty more *responsively* – by offering it at times when his bladder is full. Many parents find this style of practising the method to be intuitive and rewarding.

But how do you do this? Firstly, you can sync yourself more closely to his bodily rhythms. You have probably already been offering the potty at likely times (for example, on waking) – but by paying a bit more attention to the times he wees and poos you can start to understand his cycle better. The other way you can be more responsive is to try to respond to the signals he makes. Refer back to page 60, to recap on the kind of signals your baby might make. However, you might find difficulties if there don't seem to be any signals.

Encouraging signals

In Chapter 4 I explained why it might be difficult to recognise your baby's signals when starting out. You might find that signals disappear at this stage, or may not be present in an older baby who is used to using the potty.

Most (if not all) of the signals that we can observe in a younger baby are a direct communication of the discomfort they feel. For example, they might squirm, wriggle, cry or breathe heavily. If they don't feel discomfort, then they don't signal. As a baby gets older, the sensation of peeing or pooing may no longer feel as uncomfortable or alarming to him as it might to a younger baby. We need to remember that babies very quickly slip into associations – both towards and away from the potty. It may be that you have been offering the potty mostly based on timing, or perhaps a few out-of-sync days have resulted in more misses than usual. This is completely normal. But because babies use your reaction to guide their own behaviour, parental silence about weeing can mean they don't pay much attention to the sensation either. This means that even a couple of days of misses can result in a reduction of your baby's signals.

'Our baby uses whatever is his latest skill to signal a need to go. So when he was tiny it was fussing at the breast, then he had a special sound that we recognised, then he cried a tiny bit, then he was mysterious so we weren't entirely sure what was going on. At the moment he pinches my lip to indicate a poo, and there was a beautiful moment recently at aged eight months when he wriggled over to the potty and bashed it to signal a poo ... I was living the dream then!'

Kate, mum to Tom, eight months

'I got all the info second-hand from my wife, who avidly read various hippy parenting books. I was under the impression that the baby would learn signs and gradually be consistently clear about when he needed to go. This was absolutely not the case – even when we figured out some sign it would change within weeks. Even now, at eight months, we seem to catch stuff by magic rather than science, but he loves sitting on the potty.'

Joe, dad to Tom, eight months (and husband of Kate)

You can encourage your baby to signal by spending more time reinforcing the association between the potty (or hold) and the action of passing waste. This is simply done through repetition and drawing your baby's attention to the action. As your baby builds up the association, he will probably start to hold on to a full bladder for a moment or two, and he will start to communicate the mild discomfort he feels. You'll need to act on these communications (there will be a lot of trial and error here) in order to encourage him to hold and communicate. Remember, we are only talking here about momentary holding, not for minutes on end.

Spotting his signals

It *is* harder to pick up on babies' signals once they have moved out of the in-arms phase. This is a natural part of him growing up, and away from you. The difficulty is that the less often you respond to your baby's signals, the more likely they are to diminish.

One way of getting round this difficulty is to have more nappy-free time. Your baby doesn't necessarily have to be naked – that will probably depend on the type of flooring you have. He could wear pants or loose trousers to absorb the wee. Nappy-free time helps you to see quickly when your baby is passing waste, or if he has just done so. This is a good way of continuing to draw attention to his bodily functions at a time when he is increasingly engrossed in the world around him. This may be easier now he is spending less time on your person – as, in general, it's a lot easier to clean up the floor than your own clothes.

Making conscious signals

Although BLPT can get a bit more tricky as your baby is learning new skills and wanting to assert his independence a bit more, there are also some lovely changes while he learns to communicate more consciously.

I remember that when my little girl was a young baby, she would grizzle and act uncomfortable when she needed a wee. But after around five months, she would stop what she was doing, go very still and give me a fixed stare. At this time in her life I was very consistent about offering her the potty when she needed to go and we were catching most of her wees, so she must have had a very strong association. So, when she felt a full bladder, she had an expectation that I would take her. That's why she was looking at me – she was waiting for me to pick her up and take her to the potty. Of course, what she didn't realise is that I couldn't know that she needed a wee unless she gave me a signal. Luckily, the fixed stare was enough for me to guess.

As they get more mobile, babies can also start to signal their need to go extremely clearly. One mum told me that, if the potty was nearby, her six-month-old boy would reach over to it when he needed to go. A baby may look at the potty, or even start to crawl towards it as he gets older.

> 'She's now 10 months, and up until recently, we've not had many clear cues that anything is coming. However, in the last couple of months, she has been coming over and patting me just after she has done a wee, and this is gradually moving to coming over in advance. She has a special little whine she uses for it!'
>
> **Kathryn, mum to Natasha, 10 months**

One early-potty-training expert suggests that we can actively teach our babies to make conscious signals. In her book *Early-Start Potty Training*, Linda Sonna recommends touching your baby's hand against the potty before potty trips and also encouraging him to look at the potty. She advises that by touching the potty it will become part of the routine, so in time your baby will gesture towards it when he needs to go.

Using baby signing

Another way to encourage your baby to consciously communicate his need to pass waste is to start using 'baby signing' or 'Makaton'. Using sign language with babies has recently gained in popularity and it is very useful for BLPT. Studies have found that babies who are exposed to signs from six months are able to produce their first sign from around eight to nine months. In contrast, children don't tend to *speak* their first word until an average of 11 months old – this is because their understanding of language develops faster than their ability to master speech.[4]

Baby signing can be an excellent communication tool for BLPT, as it means your baby can potentially 'tell' you when he needs to wee or poo much earlier than if he has to wait for his speech to develop. I started signing with both my children at around six months of age, and they both signed back to me at around eight to nine months.

'I did baby sign language with both children but my eldest never picked it up. He was very delayed in all his development, especially speech and communication. But my youngest picked up on baby sign language right away. By six months of age he would just sign when he needed the toilet. This of course also meant that when he took up crawling and didn't want to go to bed at night, he would sign he needed the toilet but he was just being cheeky and trying to find an excuse to get up out of bed!'

**Shyann, mum to Duncan, nine years,
and Hamish, four and a half years**

There are numerous baby signing classes around, but you don't have to go to these to teach your baby to sign. There are lots of videos, books and websites which can help get you started. You can stick to a conventional sign language, such as British Sign Language (BSL), or you (or your baby) can make up your own signs. In our family we adapted BSL, simplifying some of the signs so they were easier for our babies. Also, as we were normally carrying a baby in one arm, we also found it useful to adapt some of the signs that involved two hands to single-handed versions.

It's easy to teach your baby signs: start around six to seven months (though it's also fine if you start later), and whenever you think your baby has his attention on the right object, you can demonstrate the sign.

When I first began sign language with my daughter I envisioned she would be able to tell me when she wanted milk, when she was cold, when she was about to wee and so on. Of course, the reality wasn't quite like that! Although she did often ask for milk using the sign, virtually all the other signs she learnt were for animals, helicopters, trains, and other fascinations. She used them simply for the pure joy of communicating. When she learnt the wee sign, I had hoped that she would use it to signal a need to wee. She did sometimes, but more often than not she used it once she was already on the potty, at the moment that the wee came out. This was still pretty useful, so I wasn't complaining! My son didn't use the poo sign much, as poos tended to come without much warning for him. My daughter, however, would sit on the potty for a wee and then do the poo sign, so I would know that she wasn't yet finished. It was very helpful.

Signs are great fun and I really recommend trying them. It isn't an all-or-nothing approach – you can just teach the signs for poo and wee if you don't fancy doing any others. But, even if your baby does pick up sign language early, you need to think of it as just *one* of the tools in the communication toolbox. You certainly can't rely on your baby to communicate all his toileting needs by this method.

Example signs you can use for BLPT

I concentrated on just a couple of signs at first, including the sign that we used for wee.

I decided to use the American sign language (ASL) version of 'toilet' as I felt it was clearer and easier for my babies to do than the BSL sign. The ASL sign for wee is a closed fist, with thumb poking out between forefinger and middle finger. You wave the hand at shoulder height. My daughter was able to produce an approximation of this sign at around nine or ten months – her version was pretty similar to a wave.

We adapted most of the signs that involved two hands to work with one hand. However, one exception in our family was the sign for 'poo'. We used the BSL sign for 'potty': the forefinger of one hand twisting into the palm of the other hand. Somehow this really clicked with my children, and they were able to produce it at a young age (around ten months). People sometimes ask whether it's necessary to have a different sign for poo, but we found it very useful.

'My 11 month old, out the blue, has started signing "toilet" whenever a toilet, wee or poo is mentioned, plus if he farts or after he's done wee ... He does it with such a beautifully impish face ... I just find it so sweet and it makes me smile.'

Tokozile, mum to Rudy, 11 months

Taking responsibility

Up until this stage you may have mostly relied on your baby telling you when he needed to go. Perhaps you were able to pick up on his body language, even if he wasn't. However, as he becomes more mobile, your baby will often play further away, so you may have to take up a little more responsibility for this and initiate potty trips at regular times throughout the day. Although he may be moving towards a more conscious expression of the need to go – for example by touching the potty or pulling at his nappy – you can't rely on him to tell you regularly. He is too young to be given full responsibility of reading his body by himself. (In the same way, you wouldn't wait for him to crawl to the fridge before you offered him food at lunchtime.)

Avoiding pickiness

As I have said before, babies can build up associations extremely quickly. Some babies will be quite happy to poo anywhere – in their nappy, on the floor, or in a public loo – but others will become quite particular, with a preference for a certain place or position. This is fine; in fact, a certain level of association is what the BLPT method hinges on. However, if you think your baby has become so attached to pooing in the red potty, for example, that he is holding on when it is not available, then you'll need to make sure that you provide enough opportunities for him to pass a bowel movement there, so that he doesn't develop a holding habit. It's also helpful to try to encourage your baby to use other places to go when possible.

Similarly, if baby usually goes to the potty with Mum, then Dad suddenly takes him, he may find it difficult to relax with Dad. It's a good idea to try to prevent this happening by taking turns on potty duties. If this has already happened, and you want to try to change the situation, then Dad (or Mum) will need to gently build up that association again. If you are pretty sure that your baby needs to go, but he can't relax, try taking him outside or offering some kind of distraction such as a story or toy. Another possibility is if the usual parent takes him while the other parent holds his hand, for example.

It's normal to find you are having more misses while you and your baby adjust to the changes he is going through at this age. You may find that you can help get things back on track by trying to pre-empt his need to go by offering more often, especially at likely times. Spending time watching out for signals may also help.

It's likely that you'll not feel quite so in sync as you did in the earlier months. Your baby will no longer be so interested in communicating about his bodily functions. As his brain develops, it will sometimes start to override his conditioned response to the potty: this is the 'wild card' thrown into the game. Eventually, over many months of practice, this will turn into complete voluntary mastery of the sphincters (as I discussed in Chapter 2). Right now we are just beginning to see the first signs of it.

Summary

- There is a lot of change in the six-to-twelve-month period as a baby makes huge developmental leaps.
- Your baby can take an increasingly active part in the pottying process.
- Teething and developmental milestones can cause temporary setbacks.
- Solid foods can make BLPT easier as poos become firmer and wees less frequent.
- Teaching your baby the sign language for 'poo' and 'wee' can be a handy communication tool at this age.

Chapter 11

Getting Started at 6-12 Months

Although many of the instructions for getting started in Chapter 4 will apply to an older baby, there are some extra considerations when starting at this age. The first important thing to note is that an older baby will wee much less often than a newborn. Also, it's likely that the infantile reflexes that made him wee and poo when his nappy was off will have faded somewhat. So you may have to work a little bit harder to get those first few catches.

However, many cultures and societies traditionally wait until a baby is sitting up, and on solids, before they begin potty training, so please don't feel you have missed the boat. A baby of this age is generally calmer, and most parents feel more confident handling him. He can sit independently on the potty around this age (perhaps with a little support to prevent topples), which can feel easier to manage as parents can have their hands free to find wipes and such like.

'The first catch was the first time I popped him on to the potty! He seemed to grasp it even though we started later [at seven months].'
Chelsy, mum to Theo, 12 months

Step one: Introduce the potty

Just as with a younger baby, the first step is to introduce your baby to the potty. You can also use the toilet with a reducer seat. (See the troubleshooting section on page 161 if your baby seems reluctant.) I also recommend getting your baby used to being held in the basic squat position, as this is extremely versatile; it will mean that you can help him to wee anywhere: over public loos, outside over nettles or over a nappy.

Of course, you'll need to take your baby's nappy off. That sounds so obvious, but for some parents it can be a real hurdle. If you find yourself hesitating for whatever reason, plan to offer the potty at a time when your baby is already naked, for example when he is about to have his bath, or when you are changing him.

Get everything ready in advance: if you plan to offer the potty when you are changing him, have the potty right next to the change mat, or have it in the bathroom if you plan to do it before his bath. A baby over six months will appreciate having toys to play with during potty time. You can even set up a stool in front of the potty to make a perfect 'table' for all his toys. An older baby will be able to reach to the floor and sit up straight again, so adjust the set-up according to the needs of your own baby.

Having your baby naked for a longer stretch and offering him the potty a number of times will probably result in faster progress. But do watch him carefully and choose lulls in his play or natural transition times to offer the potty so he doesn't feel interrupted. For example, you could sit him on the potty just after a feed. Or you could introduce a new toy right next to the potty and encourage him to sit on the potty while he explores the toy. It's also a good idea to dress your baby in very easy-access clothes, especially in the first few days of trying the method. See Chapter 5 for some ideas.

Step two: Get catches and learn patterns

So now you need to start getting some catches! If you are holding your baby over the loo or putting him on the potty at any old time, you might get lucky. Lots of parents get a catch straight away; others will have to offer 10 times before they get one. However, you'll have a better chance of getting a catch if you offer either when he's likely to pass waste due to his routine, or when he's making discomfort signals.

Using timing to predict wees

Go back to Chapter 4 and read through the section on 'Making use of predictable times', for a full summary of common times to pass waste. These will be especially useful. Your baby will almost certainly wee just after waking from a nap, so this is a really good one to go for. Sometimes it can be hard to know how quickly to put your baby on the potty or hold him out when he is still bleary-eyed from sleep. It's easiest if he isn't wearing much, or if any poppers are already undone before he goes to sleep. As I've mentioned before, babies seem to hold on a bit when they are pressed up close to your body, for example in the sling or on your hip, so you can hold him like this for a moment or two while he wakes up, and hopefully he won't wee just yet. Then, when you think he is ready, you can give it a try.

In my experience, most babies seem to like to be held out – e.g. over the sink – more than being put on a potty, especially when they've just woken up, but you'll need to experiment with this. Babies often wee more quickly in the hold than on a potty too.

Another good time to go for is a few minutes after milk. You can start to get a sense of how long it takes for milk to pass through his body, and start offering accordingly.

Making a note

Start to keep tabs on your baby's usual patterns for weeing and pooing. Be prepared that these may change, however. The process of getting used to the potty will almost certainly have some effect on your baby's weeing and pooing behaviours. For example, it is common for babies to wee and poo less often when they are using the potty. Some babies wee much more often when they are naked, and some wee more frequently when they are wearing a nappy.

Start to get a sense of what *your* baby does. Some people find that they can just make a mental note of these observations, but others prefer to actually write them down. If you keep a book or other record of your baby's special milestones, then this could make an extra-special addition that will bring back a lot of memories when you discover it years later! But how you do it is completely up to you. It is also possible to get apps that will help you keep track of your baby's patterns.

Watch out for signals

You should also start to notice if your baby displays any particular behaviours before passing waste. These might be discomfort signals of some kind or another, or they could be more conscious signs. But don't worry if you can't spot any for now – I'll discuss this further in the troubleshooting section on page 160.

Appropriate places

If your baby still wees when you take his nappy off, he may still have the reflex that triggers urination (see page 189), or he may just prefer to wee in the open air.

How do you react when he does? In most families, weeing during change times causes a fair degree of alarm: 'Oh no! You weed on Daddy's best suit/in my eye/in my tea!' This is a perfectly natural reaction to a surprise spray, but unfortunately it can send a message to a baby that it is not appropriate to wee when the nappy is off. Try to be positive about open-air wees. Being sterile, their wees are pretty harmless. It's a lot easier to be positive when they land in the potty!

Step three: Establish the connection

Now you need to teach your baby that the potty (or loo or hold) is the appropriate place to go. You can do that by helping him make an association between the act and the place. It's best to draw his attention to the wee or poo at the moment it's happening, or immediately after, while he is still experiencing the sensation. Otherwise he might not know what you are going on about. If he is sitting on the potty, it can sometimes be hard to see exactly when he starts to wee. If possible, squeeze your hand underneath the potty to feel if it is warm.

With an older baby it may take a little longer to build up the association between weeing and the potty. You may find that naked observation time is more useful with an older baby. (Training pants, or cloth nappies without a cover, are also good alternatives, though they are not quite as good as him being naked – for more clothing suggestions, see Chapter 5.) The feedback your baby will get from both noticing his own wee, and you reinforcing it with words and taking him to the potty/holding him out, will help him build up an awareness of the sensation of urination.

If you notice your baby weeing on the floor – quickly scoop him up and carry him to the potty. It sounds obvious, but it's really important that you do this in a positive manner. It's fine to express surprise or urgency in the moment you notice the wee ('Ah! /Stop!/Hang on!'), but make sure you smile and maybe have a little joke about it as you get him on the potty.

Naked babies increase our motivation to try the potty, as we have everything to gain from a catch; it's easy to hesitate and be a bit lazy when your baby is wearing a nappy. It will also help you become more aware of your baby's patterns. But if you find yourself getting stressed about misses on the floor, then it's better if your baby wears training pants, or trousers without a nappy, so you don't get any puddles.

Keep persevering

You may find that you keep missing the critical moment. Or you try your baby on the potty, but nothing happens. Don't worry! Think back to the common times that babies wee that I mentioned earlier: when undressed, upon waking, coming out of a sling or car seat, after a feed and more often in the morning (see pages 53–7 for more on this). Try putting your baby on the potty or be on the alert at these times. You may need to really put your mind to this over a day or two. But if you do that, it won't take long. I promise!

> *'I'll never forget my first poo catch with my son when he was nine months old (we'd just started). I whisked him away from his lunch at a café as soon as he made a face, and when I held him over the loo he was still holding a sausage in his fist. We watched the poo coming out together (he was craning forward to see) and he held up his sausage, which looked very similar to the poo. He looked first at it and then down at the emerging poo and back again, and we both laughed and laughed – our first poo joke together!'*
>
> **Anna H, mum to Tristan, 22 months**

Gaining voluntary control

A baby under six months releases the bladder and bowel through reflex and conditioning. However, as a baby starts to grow, the frontal lobes in his brain develop and in time this process will start to become voluntary. This will become more apparent after 10 months, so you may start to see it happening in this six-to-twelve-month period.

Starting to acquire voluntary control means that your baby can also be encouraged by praise and enthusiasm from you. (Earlier than six months, he may enjoy your delighted smiles or cheers, but it won't have much effect on how he 'performs'.) Some parents don't feel comfortable offering praise for something as 'functional' and everyday as using the potty. Others wonder if praise could 'rob' their baby of his ownership of the process. I think there is a difference between calculating praise designed to achieve certain behaviours, and genuine, shared enthusiasm that your baby is getting it right. It's completely up to you how you handle this, but I would suggest that as a rule of thumb you should keep your responses consistent with the way you parent in other areas. Also, be prepared to experiment to find out what feels right for you and your baby!

Troubleshooting at 6–12 months

'I can't get any catches'

Sometimes it does take a little while, and a little luck, to get started. Persevere. Check to see if you are making things as easy as possible for yourself. Sometimes parents can feel disheartened at the beginning and find that they are only offering half-heartedly. Really give yourself the best chance you can.

Spend some more time with your baby nappy free. A great way to do this is to have your baby nappy free in a sling as you go for a walk in your local area. Have him naked if it's warm, or in trousers with no nappy if not. This will really motivate you to tune in and offer him the chance to go! You can experiment with timings. Wear old clothes so it doesn't matter if he soils or wets them. Put him on the potty before you go out and as soon as you come back. You can experiment with how long to go for; perhaps 20 or 30 minutes will mean that he is ready to go for a wee – especially if he had a drink shortly before going in the sling.

'I'm getting catches based on timing, but I can't spot any signals'

An older baby, who has got used to weeing in his nappy, may not pay as much attention to the sensation of a full bladder. This will mean that he is unlikely to hold his bladder and therefore probably won't give off much of a signal that he is full. You may find that after a while of offering the potty and building up an association, he does start to hold on a bit and display signals of discomfort. I talk more about this feedback cycle on pages 62 and 63. He may go straight to making conscious signals, such as gazing at you or touching the potty – for more on this see pages 147–8.

Some babies go for many months without making signals. Your baby will eventually, but in the meantime you may need to stick with offering through timing and routine.

'My baby refuses to sit on the potty'

If your baby is resistant to sitting on the potty, try to work out why. Is he scared of the potty? Has he built up a negative association? If so, why might that be? Try to think how you could make potty time more attractive for him. Having older children demonstrate using the potty may help, as may offering lots of toys, especially on a little stool or table in front of him while he uses it.

It may be that your baby is going through an intense developmental stage right now, and only wants to stand or crawl. You may be able to accommodate his inclination, by, say, letting him wee standing up outside or in the bath, or you may need to wait until this period passes. Don't press the issue if it's making him unhappy, but do keep checking back every now and again, as babies change very quickly.

'How long should my baby sit?'

My rough rule of thumb is that you can keep your baby on the potty, or hold him out, for as long as you are both comfortable. If he has had a dry nappy for over an hour, or he's just had a feed and hasn't weed yet, or he's grunting and going red in the face – in short, if you have a pretty good reason to expect some kind of offering – then go ahead and keep him there as long as he's happy to sit.

When babies are just learning the ropes (especially older babies, who may have lost the reflex to wee when squatting) they don't yet know what the potty is for. So, although your baby needs a wee or a poo, he may not be relaxed enough to wee in this strange new manner.

Play with him, sing a song, share a book. If you are outside, show him the leaves and point out the birds, as you hold him out. Keep him amused and soon he will relax and do his wee. Draw his attention to it: 'Hooray! A wee!' And then – hey presto! – he is well on his way to establishing that connection.

'My baby wants to sit on the potty all day long'

Some babies really like sitting on the potty. This can be especially true if your baby has just learnt to sit and is enjoying the new perspective on life. If he wants to sit on the potty for 25 minutes – then that's fine – as long as it's convenient for you.

I think some parents feel anxious about this because they worry that they are coercing their baby to spend half his waking hours on the potty. They may be concerned about how it would look to other people (parents can worry about this even if they are doing it in private, in their own home!) They suspect that the whole method only works because their baby sits for so long that, by the law of averages, he *must* do a wee in that length of time. There is some truth in that at the beginning: we do need an element of luck and patience to get those first few catches. But please don't worry about this! I can assure you that this phase does not last very long! Once babies have established the connection between the hold or the potty and passing waste, most babies tell their parents *very quickly* when they have had enough or if they don't want to go – often within a few seconds. And, anyway, once a baby has ideas about getting mobile, the novelty of sitting still will soon wear off.

'My baby is scared of the loo'

This is quite a common experience. My little girl enjoyed sitting on the toilet with a reducer from around five to nine months. However, at that point she suddenly got very scared of the loo; nothing could entice her to sit on it, and she often refused to be held over it. I think that at this age she suddenly got a sense of heights, and probably a stronger sense of herself too – and along with that, a sense of potential dangers towards herself. Her fear of the toilet lasted a long time. She was around 15 months when suddenly, in a public toilet, she said the word 'loo' for the first time. And thereafter she was happy to sit on it. I don't have any particular answer to this conundrum. You may be able to reassure your baby that it is perfectly safe, or you may just have to wait it out.

Summary

- Six to twelve months is a good age to start BLPT, as babies can sit up and will now be on solids.
- It can sometimes be harder to get those first catches. You may need a little bit more perseverance.
- Make things easy for yourself by having your baby naked, or suitably dressed, and try to offer the potty at likely times.
- Make sure that offering the potty is a fun experience!

Chapter 12

Childcare

Whether it's part-time or full-time, many mothers return to work towards the end of their baby's first year. Preparing to find an alternative source of care for your child can be a pretty daunting process. Many parents have asked me if they can expect their childcare provider to offer the potty to their child, and, if they are willing, how to manage this.

All nurseries and childminders follow the government's early years foundation stage framework, which states that providers must work in partnership with parents to provide for children's individual needs. I therefore think that it is perfectly reasonable to expect your nursery, childminder or nanny to offer your baby the potty. (Nannies aren't bound by this regulation, but parents tend to find it easier to communicate their expectations to those they employ.)

'I've never reliably caught wees, but the childminder, who doesn't have her own children and had never done BLPT before, was very good at them. She tried to teach me what to read in my daughter but I genuinely think my daughter only "spoke" to the minder.'
Margaret, mum to Lily, 18 months

Hesitation

For some providers, the idea of offering the potty to a baby will be entirely new to them. They may even believe that it's not in the best interests of your child. Don't immediately hold this against them –

you may have held the same beliefs not so long ago. Instead, you can explain what you are doing and why, and how they can help out.

It will help if you give the care provider a brief outline of the process. Give them the key facts and also an outline of what it means in practical terms. Keep it short; they won't have time to read a whole book! (You can download a one-page summary specifically aimed at BLPT for childcarers on my website, www.nappyfreebaby.co.uk.) Explain that your baby is used to using the potty, and you feel that continuity of care in this area will help him transition to a new setting. It may be that your provider surprises you by taking it in their stride – they probably have lots of experience of dealing with potty training children.

Practicalities

If your childcare provider agrees to offer the potty, you can discuss with them how best to do this. Perhaps the easiest way for them to manage will be to offer the potty on a sensible routine. This could be at every nappy change, on waking from a nap, some time after food or drink and after certain time periods. You can ask your baby's key worker to make a note of the times that they offer. Parents often report that once the nursery staff start getting catches, they can become almost as excited about it as the parents!

Make it clear to the carer(s) that they shouldn't pressure your baby, and they should take him off if he objects to the potty. If he is making clear signals at this stage that he wants to use the potty, perhaps by signing, speaking or going to the potty, his key worker may even be able to respond on cue.

Make sure you send your baby to nursery wearing the best clothes for the job. Dungarees and vests are not conducive to regular nappy checking or offering the potty. If your baby is pretty reliable at home, you may want to consider sending him to nursery in cloth training pants. Because they don't fully contain misses, this could provide an added incentive to the staff to offer him regularly and change him when he's wet or dirty. However, you should discuss this with his key worker first, as it may add too much pressure.

> 'The nursery have done a fantastic job and have even asked me to talk to their staff about BLPT on their next training day. They have caught lots of my baby's eliminations. The nanny has been less successful. She's been looking after him regularly for over six months and hasn't caught anything, which is difficult for us.'
>
> **Becky, mum to Arthur, 12 months**

Your expectations

However co-operative your childcare provider seems to be, you need to keep your own expectations realistic. In a new, exciting environment, especially if there are lots of children to watch and interact with, your child is likely to be less interested in his bodily functions. Even if he signals clearly at home, he may not communicate in the same way to his new carer(s). Also, whatever age he enters childcare, he will be changing and developing. As I discussed in Chapter 2, at around 10 months or so he is beginning to acquire voluntary mastery of the sphincters. Sometimes his conscious effort will interfere with his conditioned response, and pottying can seem more haphazard at this age.

Of course, his carer(s) will not be so tuned into your baby as you are. They will not be able to recognise the subtle changes in his body language in quite the same way as you, and they may also have their attention divided by the other children in their care. Occasionally you may collect your child to find he has a soiled nappy. This can be disconcerting. It doesn't, however, necessarily mean your child is being neglected. Try to get a sense of how your child interacts with his carer(s). If it seems to be a warm, loving environment, the occasional miss isn't going to matter.

Refusing to co-operate

Some providers, however, don't seem to want to co-operate with BLPT at all. Perhaps they argue that it will take too much time, that there is no hygienic area for them to offer the potty in his room or that they don't believe it's the right thing to do. It's really important that you feel confident in your childcare provider. If they are being inflexible about this matter, how does this make you feel about other areas? Are you reassured that they will listen to your wishes regarding food, milk and nap times – and everything else? Will they generally respect your baby's needs? If you feel completely happy with them in every other respect, then it may be that it is worth backing down on this, in order to get the best care for your child. Perhaps there is a special advantage in choosing this provider – for example, if it is a crèche attached to your work, or if the carer in question is your baby's grandmother and her unwillingness to offer the potty is offset by the love she clearly exhibits. These are the kinds of difficult questions you need to consider when you are finding an alternative carer. There is no one right answer.

'My mum was completely sceptical about the whole thing and thought that any success we'd had was all down to timing and luck. That is until the first time she looked after Elliott all day by herself. He was sat on her lap and started to pee, but stopped himself almost instantly. She took him to the loo and he finished it there. She was so astounded that he could actually control it that she told me about it as if she had made a major scientific discovery! You really can't believe it until you see it for yourself. From then on she was much more supportive – and grateful never to have to clean up dirty nappies.'

Rosie, mum to Elliott, 23 months

Although it's better to be consistent, your baby will soon be able to learn that he doesn't use the potty at nursery or at the childminder's. He may be used to going in his nappies at other times anyway – perhaps at night, or when out and about. Make sure you send him in disposables or very absorbent cloth nappies with a stay-dry liner, in order to guard against nappy rash. You could ask for him to be changed more regularly as a concession, if you think this would help.

Even if your provider has refused to co-operate at first, keep asking at intervals. If he is at a nursery, for example, staff may be more receptive to the idea once he has moved into the 'toddler room', with other children who are potty training. If he is very reliable at home, and you think they could manage the odd accident, you could even just send him in cloth training pants, or even normal pants, and declare him 'potty trained'.

'We found nursery hard as they weren't prepared to take her to the toilet as she was too young and they couldn't have potties in the baby room. We had to wait till she moved up a group in nursery before they would take her to the toilet at 18 months.'

Mel, mum to Emma, 20 months

Summary

- It's perfectly reasonable for you to request that your baby's caregiver tries to meet his toileting needs.
- If the caregiver is unco-operative, consider whether you can trust them in other areas of care.
- If it makes sense to use a carer who is unwilling to offer the potty, then don't worry: your baby will adapt to different rules in different places.
- If the caregiver won't offer the potty, keep asking at intervals. All toddlers need to use the potty at some point.

Chapter 13

Moving Towards Toilet Independence (12–18 Months)

As a rough rule of thumb, we can say that the first year of BLPT concerns keeping a baby dry and clean. Although we pick up on signals from the baby, it is the caregiver's responsibility to ensure that his toileting needs are met, whether by helping him on to the potty, or by changing a wet nappy. For most parents who continue using BLPT during the baby's second year, they find that there is a natural change of emphasis. Now, we start to look towards a longer-term goal – moving towards toilet independence. Our job as parents is to help a baby acquire the skills he needs, so that ultimately he can take charge of this matter for himself.

As you can imagine, this is not a quick transfer. You may have sown the seeds for toilet independence when your baby was as young as six months old, or even younger, but you will still need to support him to recognise and act on his needs throughout his second year, and probably into his third year.

Changes around the first birthday

Independence
Parents tend to find there is a significant advance in a baby's sense of self around the first birthday, often coinciding directly with learning

to walk. As Dr T. Berry Brazelton (best known for his advice to delay potty training, as mentioned in Chapter 1) noted, at this stage babies divert a huge amount of their developmental energy towards becoming upright and mobile.[1] Your baby may feel compelled to practise standing at literally every opportunity possible. At this point he will also start to assert his independence and pursue his own activities. Suddenly, a baby has his own ideas about what he does and how he wants to do it, and trying to impose your will on top of his can lead to extreme reactions. You will find yourself having to adapt your old ways of interacting with your baby to meet these changes.

If this is your first child, it may come as quite a surprise that your baby may now suddenly be in opposition to you. This is a time for development in your relationship with him. Whereas before you simply gathered him up when it was time to leave the playground, now you may have to persuade him. Once he is walking, he will be able to access dangerous and unsuitable objects and places, and you'll frequently need to thwart him. His 'wants' no longer equal his 'needs', as they did when he was a baby, and sometimes you have to look beyond his wants to provide for different needs – the needs to be safe, secure and healthy. It can be challenging to work out when you should say 'yes' to your toddler, even if you would rather not, and when you should say 'no', even if you hate to limit him.

Communication leaps

Around the time of his first birthday, your child will also make great leaps with communication. It may be that he will not learn the words 'wee' or 'potty' for another few weeks, but he will be able to communicate on this subject far more effectively. If you are doing baby signing (see pages 148–51), you will probably see big strides at this time. Although some children can produce a bit of sign language from about eight months, signs will start coming thick and fast from around 12 months. So if you haven't already taught your baby the signs for wee and poo, this is a good time to do it. Other children use gesture – pointing to or picking up the potty, or tugging at their nappy, or some other unique body language. You may also still notice bodily signs of him being uncomfortably full, but these may be harder to spot as your toddler plays further away.

'At around 14 months my son was signing for the potty.'

Anna, mum to Harry, three years,
and Skye, four months

'I had a lovely couple of dry days with Theo waiting for the potty. I didn't think things could go any better as he is 12 months old and I thought we were just having a lucky few days! Well ... I was at my mum's earlier and he was pottering about. He went to where we keep the potty, picked it up, plonked it by my feet and stood patiently by it! I asked him if he needed a wee-wee and popped him on. He did a big old wee, then stood up and carried on playing! Me and Grandma were very pleased and excited! We started at seven months and days like today make it all so worth it!'

Chelsy, mum to Theo, 12 months

Unreliable pottying

The period when your baby learns to stand and walk usually coincides with him having less of a conditioned response to the potty. This means that the in-arms hold or potty will no longer immediately trigger a wee if his bladder is full enough. His brain's active role in the process is far more important. Now, he needs to learn how to consciously release the external sphincter and the pelvic floor.

It is usual for babies to become more unreliable with pottying during this period. Learning full mastery of the sphincters and pelvic floor can be a difficult and complicated process. When early potty training was standard practice in the UK, mothers reported that 12 months could be a challenging age. In *Patterns of Infant Care in an Urban Community*, written in 1963 by John and Elizabeth Newson, we can see that babies of 12 months typically sat on the potty for several minutes, then would wee immediately after they got up. Modern parents report similar stories. This can feel frustrating to parents when, until recently, their babies have been very reliable. The Newsons found that this routinely caused anger among the mothers. Their book contains the following statement from 'Mrs Lander, a driver's wife'[2]:

> 'Yes, it's a lot of trouble. I'm a bit worried about it really. That is where he really is a problem. After all, he must know what his potty's for by now – and yet I've sat here with him for half an hour sometimes, and then he'll go and fill his pants. That makes me mad. Well I suppose he'll come to it eventually, but I do worry about it – yes.'

Similarly, a 'tobacco worker's wife' said[3]:

> 'Well, when the twins were tiny, they were ever so good; but lately I can't get them to do anything for me at all. They don't like sitting on the potty, either of them. I started soon as I came home [from hospital]; and I really got them ever so clean; but as they got older … they're very obstinate now. Some days you can just put them down with a clean nappy and then they start. In fact, I gave John a tap for that yesterday. Because I'd been holding him out for ages – and in the finish I put his nappy on, and blow me if he didn't go and fill his pants as soon as I put him down, next minute. I gave him a little tap for that – because I feel as if they understand, don't you think so, a year old? I think they know, because they know what they're supposed to do now.'

In many cases, the 1963 mothers felt that their babies were being wilfully perverse. In the past, this often led to conflict between mothers and babies, and this was the main reason Dr Brazelton argued for a delayed start to toilet training.

Don't fall into this trap of becoming frustrated! We need to understand that during this period what might seem to be a 'regression' or, in the tobacco worker's wife's words, being 'obstinate', is in fact a developmental change. As the frontal lobes in his brain develop, your child will begin to override the conditioned response to the potty or the hold. He needs to learn how to *consciously* co-ordinate the muscles. At first, he has no idea what he is doing. He may not even realise that he is squeezing the sphincter shut, and it may take him a while to work out how to release it. He is not being wilfully perverse. Perhaps, as he sits on the potty, he wonders why there is no wee or poo coming out. The diminishing of the conditioned response and the acquisition of voluntary control is a gradual process, and at times one has more influence than the other.

It will take some time before your baby has complete mastery of the sphincter. Sometimes you can help him along by guiding him. Sometimes you can distract him into relaxing, and letting the conditioned response take over. You'll need to exercise patience until he has gained mastery of this physical and social skill.

Learning appropriate places

Newly toddling babies may also need help learning where they *should* put their waste. Although your baby may have previously shown signs that he enjoyed using the potty, the actual act of releasing was a conditioned, even automatic, response. Now that he is starting to walk (or almost), he has a choice about where to pass waste, and he may not know that the potty is the 'correct' place. As your toddler develops a sense of self, he will need to explore boundaries and will sometimes experiment with going against your wishes, to see what happens. This is an important part of the learning process too, and we need to provide sensitive and gentle guidance. If you introduce conflict when he is unable to co-operate, due to his physical limitations, then it is very likely to make the problem worse.

Potty pauses

It seems that the moment babies take their first steps is accompanied by major brain development, and a growth in their sense of identity. Toddlers need to assert themselves and sometimes this results in resistance to the potty. Parents sometimes refer to these as 'potty pauses', 'potty strikes', or even 'my toddler runs screaming into the other room if I suggest using the potty'. It can be hard to know how to respond to this. Perhaps, up to now, you have enjoyed a harmonious first year by following your baby's lead in most aspects. But now, even the slightest suggestion of potty time meets with a rageful response.

Whether or not your toddler goes through this phase will depend on his personality, and, to some extent, how you react to his behaviour; without meaning to, we can occasionally make things worse. Some children take the battle head-on; some just occasionally offer resistance; some co-operate all the way through. Parents whose children are more resistant may find themselves questioning whether offering the potty is the right thing to do. If, for much of the first year, it seemed that your baby was showing a distinct preference for the potty but now he is clearly saying no (even if you can plainly see he has a full bladder), you find yourself in a dilemma.

'I think the hardest thing was with my first child, going from catching every wee at around nine months, to the standing phase and having no idea why she was refusing to go on the potty. It was hard because no one had written about it honestly, and I didn't know anyone who had gone through it.'

**Antonia, mum to Miffy, seven years,
and Steffan, three years**

To continue or not?

The question of whether to pursue a potty agenda in the face of resistance, is, of course, completely up to you. From our adult's perspective, there are still advantages for pursuing BLPT, even if your toddler himself no longer delights in the experience. It still saves nappies, which means less cost and less landfill, reduces likelihood of nappy rash and so on. Also, whether or not your toddler uses the potty, you will still need to change him – and, in many cases, toddlers object to that just as much.

Tactics from overseas

In countries where early potty training is the norm, they don't give up offering the potty at this age. They know that asserting the self is a normal part of growing up, and they work around that the best they can. Of course, it is much easier for them to carry on, compared to us in the West, as their society supports them and there is a vast wealth of knowledge and experience in the community.

According to a 2013 study,[4] modern Vietnamese mothers use a variety of tactics to teach their 12-month-old toddlers bladder skills, and to keep them dry:

- Listening when the child communicates his need
- Watching out for distinctive body language
- Reminding him to use the potty many times
- Following a routine that accommodates his needs (before and after sleep, after food and then hourly)
- Not using nappies or too many clothes
- Employing lots of patience
- Offering the potty before and once during the night
- Using whistling to initiate and support peeing

Their children are generally dry at 18 months, and entirely independent by 24 months.

If conflict seems irresolvable, some parents prefer to abandon the potty altogether and pick it up again at a later date. This may be the best solution for you. The enormous benefits you have gained – the increased confidence and communication, the nappies saved – none of that will be lost if you stop now.

Some parents don't want to give up, but are unsure how to continue. There is a lack of support and communal experience in how to deal with such setbacks. We are so often told that babies can't potty train before 18, or even 24 months, that we lose confidence in their abilities – even when we've witnessed it ourselves for months!

> 'Not being goal-orientated is the hardest part. Our culture is all about results and success, and you have to measure that in a different way with BLPT. It is hard to trust in the process when you have never seen or heard of it before and don't know anyone else who has "succeeded" at it. It's hard to let the "misses" go and not to feel like a failure when it doesn't work.'
>
> **Rosie, mum to Elliott, 23 months**

Why potty battles are unique

Perhaps you are experiencing challenging behaviour in other areas, such as bedtime, at the dinner table or when getting ready to go out or leave an activity. In lots of areas, you can adjust the situation so that the issue does not come up. For example, if your toddler dislikes the buggy, you might stay close to home for a day or two, or just walk. Or, if he pulls ornaments down, you can put them on a higher shelf. At times, you may be prepared to let your child take total control of when and what he eats, or when he goes to bed.

These sorts of everyday ways of preparing the environment for your child become second nature: they help to keep the peace and allow you to give freer rein in a controlled environment. They give everyone a break and a chance to calm down. Such strategies are not 'giving in': they are about making a pragmatic assessment of the situation, and choosing battles wisely. Preparing the environment, and letting some misbehaviour pass, allows you to avoid situations where you have to say 'No' too often, or 'You must do such and such'. It can lead to a more harmonious atmosphere, and less resistance in other areas.

The difference with BLPT, however, is that the need to urinate and defecate, and the need to change soiled nappies, doesn't go away. You have to keep on addressing the issue many times a day. This can feel overwhelming for your toddler.

Strategies for potty resistance

You will probably need to use different strategies at different times, and you will get a feel for which ones are more appropriate for your child and your style of parenting. Take a look over the following suggestions and see which ones chime with you. This is a time for adapting the way you respond to your growing child, and you will almost certainly find yourself adopting new strategies and tactics that you had not considered before.

Offer choices

Children often respond well to the choice of two options – the red potty or the blue one; inside or out; with Dad, or with Mum. If your child is feeling powerless, this kind of choice may help him to feel a little bit more in control, without you having to give up on your agenda.

Make it attractive

Make potty time really fun by offering new experiences on the potty. If potty time is less interesting than the activity you have asked him to break away from, then he can start to see the potty as a punishment and may build up a negative association with it. Be generous with toys, stories, games and especially your attention while he sits on the potty. Some parents worry this is a behaviourist approach to childcare, so they aim to make the potty experience neutral. The problem here is that 'neutral' is often difficult to achieve; given that, it's far better to err on the side of 'positive' than inadvertently making the experience 'negative'.

> *'Once the children are more mobile I find it useful to have a little basket of books and toys next to the potty, to keep them interested for long enough.'*
>
> **Annina, mum to Karl, 22 months**

Go outside

Babies and toddlers alike seem to respond really well to being held outside. They are often able to relax and 'perform' much more quickly, presumably because they allow the conditioned response to kick in. 'Watering' the trees to make them grow has always been a big hit with our children.

Set up rituals

Children really enjoy special rituals. (Think about birthday candles and hanging up Christmas stockings!) You probably already have lots of rituals in place without realising. Perhaps you always give them the same plate at dinner, or you say the same words each night at bedtime, or play the same games in the bath. Does your child like pressing the button at the pelican crossing? Children really relish this type of consistency and look forward to participating in well-loved rituals. These are the types of experiences that help them to feel safe and secure and allow them to flourish in their development.

The potty is an excellent place to have a ritual. It could be choosing a sticker to stick on each time he sits, or singing a special song together, or reading a particular book. Your toddler may enjoy choosing potties, emptying and flushing the contents and the cleaning-hands ritual. He may also spend 20 minutes playing with the taps and plug at the basin.

Use play therapy

If you feel that the potty has become a real battle of wills, then it may be worth helping your child explore his frustrations through play. Lawrence Cohen's wonderful book *Playful Parenting* shows us how useful it can be to draw inspiration from play therapy. Possibilities here might be to have teddy protest about going on the potty. Or blowing a raspberry at it. Or the dolls might misunderstand the use of the potty and use it as a hat. The trick is to observe your child intently while introducing this play theme. If he is laughing and joining in, then it's probably helpful. If he is getting cross, then you may have overdone it.

Change the dynamic

Ask yourself, how do *you* feel about potty time? Are you relaxed, or are you preparing for a battle each time? Listen carefully to your tone of voice and see what message it is conveying. You may be saying, 'Do you need a wee?' but your tone of voice may be making it an accusation. He is sure to answer, 'No!' to this. I often find that having a fresh look at a situation, and coming up with some ideas to make improvements, does wonders to my *own* attitude towards difficulties. I feel more positive and confident in my position, and my children pick up on this. This is probably more important than the tactics I am making use of.

Be outwardly positive

This is such an obvious one, but a surprising number of parents don't make use of it. If you are pleased that your toddler has sat on the potty – then show him! If you can, try to join in with his delight with eye contact and smiles, and share yours, without going over the top. Make it genuine – a brisk 'good boy' doesn't have the same effect. Remember, he is trying to learn a new skill here – *voluntary* mastery of the sphincters. It's not always easy, and he'll need your encouragement.

Try a more responsive approach

I have noticed that difficulties are more likely in the second year if parents have been following a mostly adult-led, timing approach. This may have worked fine while their baby was young and co-operative, but once he is asserting his independence, he can't see why Mum wants to whisk him off to the potty at any old time. In general, children seem happier about going on the potty if *they have initiated the trip*, or if they can *feel the sensation* of needing to go. Try to shift towards a more responsive approach. Offer the potty at times when your toddler is acting uncomfortable. You may need to help him increase his own awareness, and encourage him to hold on a little bit longer, so that he begins to notice the sensation building up. This will involve a period of higher input from you, in terms of observing him, preferably when he's naked.

Introduce routines

Setting regular times for potty or toilet visits can help establish a tradition of co-operation (just like at bedtime or tooth-brushing). It can also set up good habits for future years. For example, a potty visit immediately on waking in the morning, and last thing at night before bed, are sensible times to introduce regular sits. The point is to introduce a habit – whether or not you get a catch is not so important as getting your child accustomed to sitting then. Other times could be before a mid-morning snack, or when leaving the house. Some families refer to a 'magic wee': one that the child can't feel, but comes out anyway!

In *Early-Start Potty Training*, Linda Sonna points out that our grandparents and great-grandparents also followed regular eating and drinking schedules. Some families find the idea rather alien, but children themselves usually love routines. They are likely to follow them at preschool, school and work. I find it difficult to establish this kind of routine myself, but I can see it can help ensure basic needs are met in a busy family. It will also encourage urination at predictable times.

Stop badgering

Don't keep mentioning the potty, or your toddler will feel harassed. I am sure that this is a *major* cause of resistance. Remember that your child's bladder capacity is growing, so he may not need to go as often as before. From the point of view of encouraging co-operation, it is much better to have a miss than a false potty. If you feel badgering is already a problem, think about how many times your child urinates in a day, and only suggest the potty that number of times in total (regardless of whether he co-operates, or you get a catch).

Insist

At some point you may want to establish that potty use is a non-negotiable fact of life. Wait until you are pretty sure he needs to go (or until one of the set routine times), try to wait for a pause in his play or a change of activity and be decisive. Don't present it as question: 'Do you need a wee?', or he will just say no. For some children it helps to give a warning of a minute or two. 'We'll be using the potty when you've built that tower.' Then, when you are ready, devote all of your creative energy into buying his consent. Don't get distracted by other requests or activities. You may want to slip in that you will insist that he goes – as he may acquiesce more quickly if he thinks you are serious. Then, if you can, try to give some kind of concession: 'So would you like a cracker first, before your potty?' Children don't like to think that they have lost face.

I tried to be playful and kind, but ultimately I insisted that the potty was used first and last thing, and I gently, but steadfastly, refused to be involved in any other activity until it was done. Children quickly learn that this is 'the done thing', and it makes for fewer battles in the medium and longer term. I'll cover more on insisting in Chapter 15 (see pages 213–15).

Talk to him

Again this could seem obvious, but talking to your toddler about potty use – especially when the situation is calm and the potty isn't actually anywhere about, can work really well. Be careful though – young children may just understand the word 'potty' or 'wee' and take it that you are suggesting they go (which could have the effect of badgering). When talking, be really careful to 'grade' your language so that he can understand. If I said to my two year old, 'Here's the potty in case you need it' – he would still respond with a 'NO!' Even 'Here's the potty for later' would be misinterpreted. A light touch such as: 'You had a bath, then you went on the potty, then milk, and then bed,' can help children internalise the act as a normal part of life.

Teach autonomy

Being able to get on the potty by himself can be a major breakthrough. This is likely to come a little way after walking – normally around the time he learns to walk backwards (what a cute phase!) My daughter was about 14 months old when she learnt how to back on to a potty by herself. Is your potty low enough for this? Potty chairs can sometimes be too high, especially with the splash guard. Having said that, toddlers can feel really secure in them, so they have their own appeal. Experiment a little here – sometimes you can try out different potties at playgroups or other people's houses.

Try standing up

Most children like to experiment with standing up for passing waste. They've never been able to do that before! Try to allow for this. Get Dad, or an older boy, to demonstrate how boys can wee standing up. The garden is probably best for this. Girls can wee standing too. It's best if they squat, at least a little, otherwise it will probably run down their legs, though experimenting with the force may help. Pooing standing up is harder to manage, but you may be able to quickly put some newspaper or a potty below. Some children like to squat with their feet on the seat of a toilet. This is actually very healthy for the bowel. This experimental phase will probably pass within a few weeks.

If your baby is inclined to poo standing up, and does this in his nappy without you realising, then it may help to reassert the association of poos in the potty as soon as you discover a soiled nappy. You can do this by tipping it into the potty, and then doing the clean-up process with your child, without blame.

Kit out the bathroom

Make your bathroom as user-friendly for your toddler as possible. Ideally get a step in front of the toilet that enables him to climb up, or, for boys especially, to urinate while standing on it. There are some amazing contraptions on the market which include steps, seat reducers and handles. This kind of adaptation really helps your toddler to feel independent.

> 'Both of my boys, though slightly different in their development, were using the toilet independently by 17 months of age. We have a toilet-seat attachment with a built-in step that is plastic and light, and they could put it on the toilet themselves when they needed to use it.'
>
> **Shyann, mum to Duncan, nine years, and Hamish, four and a half years**

Dress for success

It's not much good if your toddler can get to the potty or toilet by himself, but he can't manage his clothes. It's far easier for him if he can move around naked at home. Perhaps dress him in baby leg warmers or socks and shoes to provide a bit more warmth. Skirts and dresses can work well for a girl, or a kilt for boys. Split-crotch trousers are another possibility (see page 89). My daughter would never wee through these, however, as she had already learnt that trousers should be pulled down! If your toddler needs to wear trousers, then he'll have the best chance with loose-fitting elasticated tracksuit bottoms. Teach him to 'push down' trousers, not pull down, and show him how to push them down over his bum. It's unlikely he'll be able to manage this before 18 months, however, and probably a lot later.

Be patient

Whatever strategy you take, patience and acceptance will be essential to keeping this a positive experience. Sometimes it can be hard. Please remember that this is a learning experience. While it may seem as if you are in a battle of wills at times, actually your toddler has very little control over his behaviour. With your help, he can learn how to self-regulate and manage himself in a complex world. *Try to stay on his side.* You can still assert your own agenda, but you need to be sympathetic at the same time.

> *'The hardest thing for me was when we had months of Rafi refusing to be held in the in-arms position, which had worked well for us up till then, and he wouldn't go in the potty either. Then, just after I'd tried, he would go all over the floor. I couldn't detect any signals from him at all and couldn't see a way through it. But then suddenly, when he was around 13 months, we started having loads of catches and he made up his own noise (a kind of raspberry) to mean "loo". That was so exciting.'*
> **Juliet, mum to Luca, 4½ years, and Rafi, 17 months**

Backing off

Sometimes you get the sense that it is all too much for your child (and for you). Any mention of the potty results in negative associations and conflict. I found with both my children that this tied in directly with episodes of teething. My son in particular went through extremely negative patches as each tooth emerged – about a couple of weeks for each one. His negative behaviour wasn't just limited to the potty; he would also refuse to be put on the bike seat, for example, when it was time for us to go out. He was normally very co-operative, so it was easy for me to see when he was in a black phase. At such times, it may be useful to back off.

But how can you back off when the need to be changed is still there? There are a number of ways you can do this, as outlined below. I used the first method a lot with my son.

Keeping him naked from the waist down

Obviously this can only be done at home, and occasionally in outdoor scenarios such as in the park (not playground) or on the beach. The advantage of this is that you can literally ignore wee misses, and simply clean them up from the floor. Poos can be more difficult, but I still found it easier to clean the floor. The usefulness of this method is that it often helps your toddler regain any lost awareness of his functions, and he may be more willing to co-operate with potties when the faff of clothing is removed.

Change without fuss

The other option is to avoid offering the potty, but to continue to change him when he is wet or soiled with as little fuss as possible. It's unusual for toddlers to enjoy lying down to be changed, unless parents have developed rituals and games to make the experience fun. Even then toddlers often object. This is true regardless of whether you have been offering the potty or not, though parents who use nappies conventionally have probably put more effort into finding solutions for this. It's fine to change your toddler standing up, ideally without disturbing his play.

Disposables or more absorbent cloth

The next option is to simply leave him in a wet nappy as long as possible. Disposables are so absorbent that they practically last all day. The disadvantage of this is that your toddler is very likely to lose some awareness of his functions, and when you do resume potty use again, you will probably have to put some work in for him to pick up the skill again. (Though it won't be as difficult as starting from scratch.) Also, there are all the disadvantages of increased cost, nappies going to landfill and the potential of nappy rash.

I used this technique in combination with naked time with my son for about two months shortly before he turned two. We had no washing machine due to building works. When we resumed using the potty use he was much more co-operative.

'Backing off' often involves some loss of awareness of body signals and rhythms on the parts of both the parent and child. I'll talk about how you can get this back in Chapter 15.

Summary

- The 12–18-month period is a transition time. There is a shift in emphasis from your role in keeping your child clean, to helping him become more autonomous in his toileting.
- Your toddler is increasingly acquiring voluntary control of the sphincters, so BLPT will seem more haphazard as he tries to exercise this skill.
- As he grows more independent, he may become resistant to using the potty.
- Be creative with different strategies to buy his co-operation.
- If all else fails you can back off for a few days or weeks, and pick it up again later.

Chapter 14

Getting Started at 12–18 Months

Forty years ago, it was standard practice to start potty training from 10 or 12 months. The good thing about starting now is that your baby's bladder will have matured considerably. He is beginning to be able to control the urethral and anal sphincters at will – both keeping them closed, and opening them. So it makes sense to start teaching him how to use that skill appropriately. Once he is practised at holding his bladder, he is likely to go much less often than a younger baby, and he will be able to hold it until you can get him to a potty. He is also more able to communicate consciously, and may even be able to tell you in words when he wants to go.

However, I think it is fair to be clear from the outset: the 12–18-month period is not the easiest time to initiate BLPT. By this age your baby has probably lost the infantile reflex which encouraged him to urinate when his nappy was taken off. By default, he may have been conditioned to wee and poo in his nappy. He may get upset if you try to move him around. He is very interested in the activities and environment around him, and less interested in the workings of his body. But he is probably not quite old enough yet to make an intellectual understanding of the potty process.

Reasonable expectations

If you want to start now, you need to make sure that you have reasonable expectations of the outcomes. Your baby has truly passed the 'golden' in-arms phase of few misses and hardly any washing – that period relies on him passing waste through a conditioned response. By now his brain's frontal lobes will be interfering with those messages as he learns to take full mastery of his body. The pottying process is likely to be long and, most probably, a bit messy!

BLPT at this age will probably work better in some families than with others. 'Success' will depend on your expectations (or how you define the term 'success'), your circumstances and the current abilities and attitude of your baby. If you define success as having your baby out of nappies with no accidents within a few weeks, then it is highly likely you will be disappointed. Your baby is not quite old enough to begin conventional potty training with conventional expectations.

I think that at this age you should define success by considering:

- Is the process fun and playful?
- Is your baby learning to make a positive association with the potty?
- Is he increasing his awareness of his bodily functions?
- Are you enjoying increased communication with your baby?
- Are you happy with the amount of misses to clean up?

It's worth bearing these in mind to check if BLPT is working for you. If you are answering 'no' to any of these questions, consider if you need to adjust your approach, perhaps by using some of the strategies in the previous chapter.

Signs that BLPT might work well

There are a number of behaviours that your 12–18 month old may exhibit which suggest he will be receptive to using the potty at this age. Have a read through and see if you recognise any of them. It doesn't matter if you don't notice any – it's just that they may give you a head start.

- **He still wees when you take his nappy off:** It's unlikely the open air still triggers a reflex to release urine at this age, but it may be possible. Even if you haven't been consciously encouraging it, some toddlers may have got into the habit of urinating at this time. If so, that will be very helpful. Or, more likely, if he has recently begun the behaviour, he may even be 'doing it on purpose'. The first thing you need to do is give him an appropriate outlet for this by catching it in a potty. If you have been making an expression of alarm or distaste, you'll need to turn your negative reaction into a positive one in order to encourage him to wee outside his nappy.

- **Your toddler waits until you put his nappy back on:** Lots of toddlers hold in a wee or poo during a nappy change and soil it a moment or two later. This is also a really good sign! It means that he is exercising bladder and bowel control already and he is also expressing a preference for where he goes. It's quite likely that he has become so accustomed to using his nappy that he holds on to waste until he is in it again. It doesn't feel right to go anywhere else. This means that he is doing the right thing, just in the 'wrong' place – it's not a massive step to teach him the 'right' place.

- **He's really interested in the workings of the toilet:** Perhaps you often find him throwing his toys in there!

- **He goes behind the sofa or another private place to defecate.**

- **He tells you when he needs a nappy change.**

- **He may even tell you when he needs to wee.**

- **He may be very co-operative and eager to please.**

- **He loves to imitate everything you (or older siblings) do.**

Alternatively, you may also be motivated to try BLPT due to challenges you are facing. He may hate having his nappy changed, or wearing them at all. Or perhaps he has very bad nappy rash, or a trouble with constipation, so you are keen to seek alternative remedies. These are all good reasons to try BLPT too.

Even if your toddler doesn't do or have any of these things – don't worry! It's worth giving it a try to see what happens anyway. The steps will be somewhat similar to starting with a child over six months of age (which I described back in Chapter 11). You'll need lots of patience, perseverance and a fair bit of luck.

Getting started, step by step

The main difference with starting with a child older than 12 months is that you will probably need to switch around the first two steps of the process described in Chapter 4. With a younger baby, it's fine to just hold him in position and pop him on the potty at any old time and hope to get a catch some time soon. However, a toddler would tire of this very quickly. Instead, you first need to help your toddler become aware of his own bodily functions and, also, *you* need to start getting a sense of his patterns.

Step one: Raise awareness of his bodily functions

Unlike with a younger baby, nappy-off time is pretty much essential when introducing BLPT at this age. You'll need to become hyper-alert to his wee patterns and any signals he might give you. And you'll need to draw his attention to his weeing too. The likelihood is that he will find it very interesting by himself. Just spending time naked and matching up the sensation with the act of weeing will help him make a strong connection.

Step two: Introduce the potty

Introduce the idea of the potty and its potential contents by having toys and teddies sit on it (you can quickly pour a bit of water in to complete the story). You can get another child to demonstrate the art – you can even wee on it yourself! Read books about children using the potty, and watch some videos on YouTube. If your child poos in his nappy, then drop the contents into the potty before you clean up. Involve him in the rituals. Toddlers often love flushing the loo and saying 'bye-bye wee!' Even if your toddler doesn't seem to be paying attention, you can be assured that he is soaking it all up, as it were.

In an ideal scenario, you will spot him mid-wee and gently but quickly transfer him to a potty. It's probably easiest to have a potty just to hand and gently guide him backwards to sit down on it. Some parents like to keep the potty in the bathroom, but in these beginning stages, I would suggest having one on hand, so as to cause minimal disruption to his play. In time you can also use the toilet or the bushes in the garden.

Be aware that your child may be nervous about the toilet, so don't insist if he seems hesitant. The bushes can work well, but if he is playing naked outside it may not be very clear to him that he needs to do anything particularly different. You could emphasise the call to action by having him wee in a certain area of the garden, for example.

Step three: Help your toddler build an association

You are likely to have lots of misses on the floor while your baby gets used to recognising the sensation of urinating. Offer the potty at likely times for a catch: upon waking, for example, or a few minutes after a drink. It's a good idea to make a note of his patterns and timings, as this will help you offer at the right times. Every time you do manage to get a catch, this will reinforce the association of weeing and pooing and the potty.

Summary

- Children older than 12 months are starting to gain control of their sphincters and can take an active part in the process.
- Although it may look similar from the outside, starting BLPT at this age is different to conventional potty training.

- The benefits of starting BLPT now will include increased communication, acquiring mastery of his body and learning how to use a potty.
- Be realistic: expect lots of misses and don't expect him to complete the learning process in a few weeks.
- There are three steps to starting:
  - o Step one: Raise awareness (both his and yours)
  - o Step two: Introduce the potty
  - o Step three: Help build associations

Chapter 15

Day Completion

Some parents think that offering the potty from birth means they 'won't have to potty train'. Although this may be true to an extent, it can also be an unhelpful way of looking at the process. These parents may find themselves using the same techniques for pottying with their 24 month old as they did when their baby was 10 months old, and then they wonder why he is 'not potty trained yet'. If you want to help your baby reach toilet independence at the end of the BLPT process, you have to adapt to your changing child. BLPT is a partnership, with you supporting your child to learn at his own pace.

Throughout the whole process of BLPT, you need to recognise when your child is at the next stage of readiness, and provide opportunities for him to develop. This is especially true as you near completion, and your toddler needs guidance to help him reach full mastery. By the end of the process, your child will have learnt how to spot when he needs to go, how to get himself to the right place and position, and how to voluntarily pass waste. Most importantly, he will have learnt that he has to do this *every time*. This is what we mean by 'completion'. He has now acquired all the skills he needs to manage his waste by himself – he is now truly toilet independent.

Some children who have practised BLPT acquire these skills seemingly without any particular effort on the part of the parent or child, or without any striking change in behaviour. They may gradually shift from assisted potty use to independence, with parents only noticing the change after it has occurred. Other children need more input. Their path may be more faltering, with setbacks and sudden leaps forward, or it may plod along on a part-time basis until their parent pulls the process into sharper focus.

> ### Similarities and differences to conventional potty training
>
> Although the BLPT completion process is not the same as conventional potty training, there are many similarities. Children who have worn nappies conventionally will have to learn the same skills. However, most conventional potty training advice is based on the assumption that you want the whole process over and done with in the shortest time possible. When we practise BLPT, however, we embrace the learning period, and we recognise that even *imperfect* potty use still brings plenty of advantages. A big benefit to offering the potty from birth is that your child can try out each new skill in his own time: he doesn't have to wait for you to guess when he is ready. In fact, your child has already acquired most of the skills necessary for autonomy, which gives him a major head start!

A gradual transition towards completion

When children make a gradual transition from BLPT to independence, the process tends to reflect the way the families have practised BLPT. The two main approaches are the 'timing approach', and the 'signals-led approach'. The following examples show how these different approaches transition towards BLPT completion.

This first example shows how the Evans family transitioned from a timing, or routine-based, approach.

> The Evans family had been used to offering the potty regularly from six months, based on a routine. Their son, Connor, was generally amenable to being held out or asked to sit on the potty. The parents picked up very few signals from Connor. They offered the potty around five times a day: on waking, mid-morning, after lunch, teatime and bedtime. By around 20 months or so, Connor's bladder matured to the point where these five trips normally met his urination needs.

In this kind of situation, parents may suddenly notice that it has been many days since a miss – and then a few weeks have passed, until they realise that their son has potty trained without them really noticing. Of course, there are bound to be times when their toddler has more to drink than usual, or the routine is disrupted, or a friend is looking after him. On those occasions, it's possible that the child will be caught unawares and a miss will occur. This is especially true the younger the toddler. However, after some time of being regularly dry, the association of the sensation with the potty will become so strong that, when he is able, he will initiate a potty trip, even if he is not ordinarily used to asking for it.

The next example shows how the transition may happen from a more responsive, or signals-led, approach:

> The Thompsons have always found their daughter Lily to be very communicative about the need to wee or poo. As a baby she would cry or wriggle when she needed to go, and as she got older her signals became more conscious. She was early to talk, and from 12–13 months she would sometimes say 'wee-wee' when she needed to go. She became less reliable during the learning-to-walk phase and seemed to want to experiment with toileting privately – often in her nappy. However, when this phase passed she became even more reliable at verbalising her need to use the potty, and by 16 months she was generally dry.

Her parents switched her to pants at this age. From this age she would rarely soil or wet herself, though she still often needed help in recognising that she had a need to go.

These examples show two different ways BLPT can seamlessly transition to a miss-free child before the second birthday. Each way has its own merits and features – one is not better than the other. However, it is important to note that, in both cases, the parents are still an important part of the process. In the first scenario, the parents oversaw and helped maintain a healthy and realistic routine. In the second, the parents let the child lead the schedule; however, they regularly acted as a safety net when their daughter failed to notice the telltale signs of a full bladder. It is likely that both sets of parents will need to assist in these roles beyond the second birthday – and possibly for longer than that.

> *'I could never read a sign from Toby when he would need the toilet; I would just offer it to him very frequently … When I see our friends struggling with potty training, and still being in nappies at three years old – phew! I'm so relieved we never had to go through that. We never had to potty train, it just happened.'*
>
> **Bianca, mum to Toby, 30 months**

When extra input is needed

For other children, the journey towards toilet independence is less straightforward. The rest of this chapter is for those children who will need a little extra input to reach completion.

In the above examples, the children learnt to use the potty reliably through sheer repetitiveness and consistency. Although the methods were different, both children had almost all of their toileting needs met at the potty. When toddlers do not have such a strong association or a tradition of using the potty – either because the parents have not prioritised this up till now or because of their own resistance – then those children may need further help.

In our family, my daughter transitioned gradually towards completion, and we took her out of nappies at 15 months. My son needed more input, and I'll tell you more about his journey on pages 206–207.

So what is it exactly that you need to do – and how is that different to what you've done before? If you think your child is ready to start learning to be consistent in his pottying, then you'll need to be consistent in your responses. (I'll show you how to recognise readiness in a minute.)

The goal of this stage is to help your toddler learn how to use the potty *every time*, and you'll need to put in a little extra time and effort to do that. You'll help heighten your child's awareness of his need to pass waste, and to reiterate and reinforce how and where to do that. It's not so different from what you've already been doing for the past year or so – just with added emphasis on guidance and support. This will be a very similar process to the one you went through at the beginning of your BLPT journey (and possibly at other times, when you were trying to get back on track after a setback or more casual period).

Is this potty training?

Some parents find it helpful to think of this stage as 'potty training'. The term recognises that we parents now have an end goal more clearly in mind (toilet independence) and that some input is needed to help our children get there. For some parents, having an end goal may feel like a big change in perspective, as prior to now they thought of offering the potty as a bonus activity, rather than as part of a wider process. Others see the completion stage of BLPT simply as a continuation of their journey so far, and they prefer to avoid the term 'potty training'. Either way is fine.

When to give extra input?

The big question of *when* to do this is the question that pre-occupies most conventional advice on potty training. The NHS Choices website, which provides guidance for potty training at a conventional age, suggests that most parents 'start thinking about' potty training from 18 months to 30 months.[1] I think this age range is also relevant for children who are already used to using the potty. A few children (generally those that transition seamlessly from assisted toileting to independent toileting) are capable of being reliably clean and dry earlier than this: perhaps between 12 and 15 months. These children may tell their parents when they need to go (though they would still need some support with their clothing, etc.), or they may happily follow a routine, which keeps them reliably dry. However, the majority of Western children are ready to learn how to consistently use the potty a little bit later: between 15 and 24 months. Also, we need to remember that children may have accidents for some weeks or months afterwards. Or they may still need substantial support from you in terms of keeping up a toileting routine to keep them dry.

You may have noticed that I just referred to misses as *accidents*. That's because, once we have initiated the completion stage, we are aiming to get all the wees and poos in the right place. Before this, misses were neutral events – an inherent part of the BLPT process. But from now on there is a 'right place' and a 'wrong place', and if wee or poo ends up in the wrong place, it's an accident. (It may be that you have already been gently guiding your baby about the 'right' or 'wrong' places to wee already – that's fine too, it's just that now you'll need to be a little more clear and consistent about that.)

Potty-training experts emphasise the idea that parents must wait until their child displays 'the signs of readiness' before starting. Because they try to offer a method which is effective in the shortest amount of time possible, they don't want parents making a false start. With BLPT, however, it doesn't matter much if you attempt to start the completion stage too early; if you find that it's not working for you or your toddler, you can simply backtrack a little and go back to what you were doing for another few weeks. Because you are aware of your toddler's toileting patterns and behaviours, BLPT allows for a much more accurate assessment of when your child is ready. You are much less likely to put pressure on too early, or to miss the best opportunity and leave it too late.

The NHS website suggests that parents shouldn't even *begin* potty training until their child shows a high level of bladder and bowel awareness, including knowing when they are wet or dirty, when they are passing urine and even when they need to go. It also suggests that you should wait until the gap between passing urine is at least an hour. I would argue that pretty much all of these signs of readiness are skills that can be learnt along the way. The question is more whether your child has the *potential* to acquire these skills – and very often you won't know until he tries. So you don't need to wait until your child spontaneously displays these skills: you can help teach them to him.

If he is around 18 months, then it's likely his bladder is potentially mature enough to hold urine for at least an hour or two. However, if he has never been asked to hold on until he is at a potty, then he may just find it easier to release little bits of urine at a time, perhaps every 20 minutes. You can teach him what is acceptable, and what isn't, and you can help him acquire the physical ability to hold through practice.

Learning through imitation

Children are born wanting to be social, and evolution has equipped them with an innate drive to imitate those around them – especially, it seems, slightly older children. Learning how to hold and release the bladder is a physical skill; in time most children will learn this by themselves, even without any input from others. Learning *where* to put the urine is a social skill: some places are socially acceptable; some are not. Although there may be an evolutionary bias towards weeing in the open air, evolution does not point us towards the toilet, rather than, say, the carpet. This needs to be learnt. If children around them demonstrate how to urinate in a socially acceptable (and accessible) way, then toddlers can find toilet training quick and easy.

Gaining toilet mastery is often much easier in traditional cultures. The following example shows how a 14-month-old Digo boy from Msambweni, Kenya, would typically transition to independence[2]:

> Mosi plays outside with his brothers, sisters and cousins for most of the day. Whenever an older boy needs to urinate, he runs over to the side of the road and wees in the bushes. If he needs to defecate, he goes and squats in the field away from the dwellings. Mosi watches this display countless times a day, from children and adults alike. As he is playing naked, he can also try copying this behaviour. When he occasionally gets it wrong, nobody minds much – it's barely even noticed.

However, in our country, we require so much more of our toddlers:

> Tommy, also 14 months, lives with his parents and his older brother, Paul, who is four, and is at school most days. Sometimes Tommy is in the bathroom when Paul uses the toilet. Paul is able to pull down his trousers and sit on the loo by himself. There is a step in front of the loo, but Tommy is not yet able to use it to climb on the loo. If he could, he wouldn't be able to pull down his trousers without help. The toilet is very high and makes a roaring noise at the end. Sometimes his parents use the toilet in front of him, and sometimes he sees adults go in the bathroom and close the door. When he needs a wee, his mother or father sometimes holds him over a bush outside, or sometimes tells him to sit on the potty. He can't remember seeing anyone else sit on the potty or wee outside. Tommy goes to a couple of playgroups in the week where he plays with children around his own age. There is a potty next to the toilet, but he has never seen any other child use it.

Children of this age are aching to act like their peers and to do things for themselves. No wonder they sometimes get into difficulty when we suggest they use the potty – they hardly ever see other children using it – let alone adults! Parents often remark that they do use the toilet in front of their child. Although that's very useful, it can't change the fact that, essentially, in our society we urinate and defecate in private, and that is very unhelpful for toilet training. The toilet itself is prohibitive for toddlers as they cannot access it without help, or even if they can, it can seem frightening and insecure. We use a potty to try to make it easier, but because no one else seems to use the potty, toddlers can't very easily pick up this skill through imitation.

Even if we practise full-time BLPT from birth, we are very unlikely to see our children potty trained to a socially acceptable level in the same timescale as children in rural Africa. Quite aside from cultural expectations, we are setting a much more difficult task. Even if you lived in some kind of alternative community, it would be very difficult to recreate the same conditions that lead to early completion in Africa.

> *'These days I often pee in the potty myself in order to inspire Hans! He's very interested in the process and laughs and smiles a lot when he sees me do it. The only tricky thing is keeping him away from the potty long enough so that I can pull up my trousers without him reaching into the potty with his hands – aaargh! But overall I think that it's helping him make a connection to the potty that will become very useful once he goes nappy free.'*
>
> **Beatrice, mum to Hans, 14 months**

Making the change

Assuming that you can't enrol a group of adults and children to regularly use the potty in front of your toddler (or even if you can), you'll need some other strategies for teaching toileting behaviour. Thankfully, you've already come a long way. Even if you have only been offering the potty occasionally, your baby still knows exactly what the potty is for, and how to put something in it. This is a tremendous hurdle already out of the way! But you still have an important job to do: *at some point in this second year, you will need to start teaching your baby that it is no longer acceptable to wee or poo anywhere else.* (Possibly with the exception of the garden!)

Here are some steps to take to help your baby reach toileting independence:

Avoid confusion

If you tell your child (either explicitly or through your behaviour) that it is fine to wee in his nappy, but if he is naked or in pants then he needs to use a potty, then that can cause confusion. Some toddlers – in fact, some babies – *are* happy to make a distinction: I have seen babies and toddlers who will hold a wee for some time when their nappy is off, but will be unconcerned about weeing in a nappy. The opposite can also be true: some babies prefer not to wee when they are wearing a nappy or any other clothing, but 'dribble' all over the place when they are naked. However, if you are trying to help your child complete their potty learning, it's much better to be consistent and teach him that he needs to act on a full bladder or bowel *every* time. This is, of course, your long-term goal.

Ditch the nappies

Up till now I've suggested that using nappies during BLPT is completely optional. Many parents like to offer the potty occasionally, and use nappies conventionally at other times. Other parents try to offer the potty as much as possible, but their baby or toddler wears a nappy as a backup between potty trips. Once you have decided to encourage independence, however, then I think ditching nappies is an important step in the process.

If you have been using nappies as a backup, you may find it hard to let go of them. They seem so practical and convenient – a much more laid-back approach, which stops you stressing about misses. That was fine before. But now, you need to respond differently to misses –

treating them as 'accidents' instead. Taking off the nappies altogether sends a clear signal to both you and your toddler. (You can still keep one on for nights, if you are using one then – I'll talk about that in the next chapter.) If you are worried about the carpet or accidents when out and about, you can use cloth training pants or absorbent trousers. Disposable pull-ups are no good as they feel the same as a nappy to your child – and, as they reliably contain any accident, it's difficult to spot misses straight away. Pull-ups are a clever way of marketing nappies to parents who are on the point of giving them up.

Make the most of it if your toddler initiates the change

Sometimes toddlers themselves initiate the change from nappy to pants, around the age of 18–21 months, even though they aren't consistent about potty use beforehand. More often than not, it is a girl who sees an older sibling or cousin using pants, and she wants to copy. But it happens with boys too. Seize this opportunity if it occurs! If you don't, it may not come round again for many months. This desire to imitate will go a long way to help with the process. You'll still need to be patient – it's unlikely that your child will grasp the full significance of wearing 'big boy pants'; he is simply won over by the picture. He'll have to learn the ropes just the same as if you have initiated the change. But his motivation will certainly make it easier.

... But don't wait for it!

A lot of parents think you *have* to wait for toddlers to express an interest in pants before you cast off the nappies. You don't. In fact, if he doesn't seem to be interested, then it's helpful to cultivate an interest in underwear. This can be a light touch – showing him the odd 'underwear' picture book, or pointing out the interesting design on the pants in the supermarket aisle. Maybe it has never occurred to him he will stop wearing nappies one day. Tell him, 'Cousin Jamie wears pants, and we'll get some for you too, soon.'

Under-twos are unlikely to be very attached to wearing nappies. After the age of 24 months, however, your toddler may get upset about giving them up. If he does display a strong attachment, it's worth trying to diminish that (with tact), as it will only get stronger during the third year. A possible way to do that might be to simply 'run out' and show your child the empty packet. Or, tell him all the cloth nappies are in the wash. Toddlers can't possibly understand the ramifications of nappy use, either on a personal level, or a global one. So, when you think the time is right, it's up to you to step in and use your superior knowledge of the way things work.

Provide guidance

Because the majority of toileting needs are met behind closed doors, you will need to provide *explicit guidance* to your child – otherwise, how will he know? He can't learn this by himself. This may be a gradual change that occurs over many months, or you may choose a day in advance. At some point you will need to explain that it is *not correct* to wee or poo in/on his nappy/clothes/the floor.

You probably provide guidance on lots of other types of behaviour. When he pulls the cat's tail, or unravels the loo roll, or throws food at Grandma, some way or other you let him know that this is not socially acceptable behaviour. I'm not talking here about telling him off. Toddlers at this age are not yet sophisticated enough to be 'naughty on purpose'. I mean gently teaching him the right way to go about things, with your face, words and gestures.

When he tries to say a word, for example, but gets it a little wrong, you show that you understand and provide feedback with the correct pronunciation. You are not making a moral pronouncement; you are simply leading him towards the correct path. When he tries to put the butter in the bin you say, 'No! Not in there. Here, in the fridge.' In short, you are continually educating your child to the intricacies of our complex social world. Toileting behaviour requires the same gentle guidance.

Shifting your role

It can be hard for parents to recognise the change in their role at this stage. Lots of parents get so used to the day-to-day activities of offering the potty and changing misses; they get so used to the 'journey', in fact, that they forget that they are going anywhere. The 'destination' of completion becomes a distant blur. I am sure that this shift in roles and responsibilities is harder with a first child; because you cannot see exactly where you are going, and how long it might take to get there, it's more difficult to keep the overview.

Some parents may worry that a shift in emphasis is a break away from the baby-led philosophy of the earlier months. I don't think so. The method is still led by the physical and developmental maturation of the child. Your child has a *need* for you to provide guidance – this is what you are led by, not just the superficial *wants* of your child. Also, most importantly, you are led by your own child's personality and stage of development: you look to him to see how best to guide him.

'We went through a difficult period from 8 months to 16 months where all pottying basically ceased. My son protested massively to any attempts to go to the toilet or potty and I was pretty disheartened. I thought that it had all been for nothing, which was disappointing. I kept talking to him about his wees or poos during this time and occasionally he would sit on the toilet. Suddenly at 15 to 16 months he started to point out when he needed to go and this awareness kept increasing until at 18 months I took the plunge and put him in pants throughout the day. I'm glad I didn't give up communicating with him through the difficult period as I think that's what enabled the awareness to remain.'

Jill, mum to Toby, 20 months

Accelerating the learning process

I think it can be very helpful to set aside some time when you can really focus on the learning process. You don't necessarily have to stay at home for three days, as some conventional potty-training manuals suggest, but I think you do need to commit a certain amount of time and space to enable the learning to happen. You'll need to be able to respond immediately to your toddler as soon as he indicates he needs to go, or as soon as he starts to pass waste in the wrong place. It's often easiest to do that when you don't have other distractions. As he already knows how to use the potty, you have got a massive head start on children who are new to the game. However, the goal now is to teach him to use it every time.

Here are some steps that can help you speed things up:

Watch your child

And I mean *really* watch him – just like you did right in the beginning. It's best if your toddler is naked. Make sure he has lots to drink. Play with him and keep watching until he makes a sign he needs to wee, or if he starts to wee on the floor. Then pick him up mid-wee and put him on a potty, so the rest of it lands inside. The same goes for poos. The objects of this exercise are:

- You relearn the signals he displays before passing waste.
- You draw his attention to the sensation of passing waste.
- You show him where to put his wee or poo by transferring him to the potty.

These ideas aren't new to your child, so it won't take long for him to catch on and understand that this is what he has to do every time he feels the sensation of a full bladder or bowel.

Respond to accidents with an impact – then a lighter touch

I took my son's nappy off for good when he was 24 months. I waited until he was weeing before I whisked him off to sit on the potty. He was so surprised, he didn't have time to object. This is what I term making *an impact*. A huge amount of learning goes on in that moment. The sudden whole-body experience, and the surprise of being lifted over to the potty, means that your toddler is completely focused on what's going on. New experiences literally make the brain connect and grow, as new synapses are forged. It's quite possible that he will make a strong connection between the sensation of weeing and the potty that very first time.

However, what happens if you keep doing that? The action is no longer a surprise, and your toddler will quickly become very fed up of the experience. There he is playing happily and you rudely grab him and plonk him on the potty. After the third or fourth time (or, if your child is unusually laid back, the thirteenth or fourteenth time), your toddler is very likely to object and may struggle, shout and try to get off the potty. This is no longer the intense learning experience it was at first; it's more likely to create a negative association. That won't help at all.

So after you have made your impact, you'll need to adopt a *lighter touch*. You still need to consolidate the learning, and you are likely to have to reiterate the new rules many times before your child has them internalised. However, now it may be enough to say, 'Oh! Potty.' Or, perhaps gently touching him to indicate that the potty is just behind him. If you notice too late that he is weeing on the floor, you may say, 'Oh dear, that should have gone in the potty, shouldn't it?'

Respond with the comic touch

If I felt my son was being overwhelmed with the new rules, then I tried to lighten it even further by adopting an exaggerated comic response to accidents. 'Oh no!' I would groan, with my hands over my face, 'not a wee on the floor … oh deary me, whatever shall we do?' My son found this hilarious. Some parents question whether this might make him actually wee on the floor on purpose, in order to generate the comic response. I don't think so. In our case this got the message across that the wee on the floor was a mistake, but that he wasn't in trouble.

I also use this technique occasionally in other areas, for example if he starts emptying the bin. Although he might enjoy continuing the game during the time that I am pretending to groan and pull my hair out, I find that he doesn't repeat the behaviour once we have moved on to something else. I think the message is still clear, but the laughter gives him a chance to process it and leaves him relaxed.

Adjust things for your child

Of course the fundamental point about all this is that you are the one who knows your child best, and you can sense whether a lighter touch or firmer guidance is required. Having said that, there will undoubtedly be a lot of trial and error involved. The trick is to try to notice when you get it wrong and adjust accordingly. If you are being quite firm and your toddler is starting to get cross and aggressive, then it may be time to lighten up.

> *'At about 20 months my son was having a bit of potty resistance so to encourage him back we started putting his soft toys on the potty and pretending they needed to wee. It was very sweet when he'd go and fetch a second potty for his toy monkey or bear to sit on next to him. Soon after this he was reliably dry day and night, which was quite a surprise, especially night-time dryness, as we'd never offered a potty at night.'*
>
> **Anna, mum to Harry, three years, and Skye, four months**

Occasionally it's worth sticking to your guns. For example, you may insist that he sits on the potty before bed, even if he is initially resistant. I'm not talking about physically restraining him on the potty – overpowering is always best avoided. A possible way of doing this is to tell him firmly that first he'll sit, and then *afterwards* he'll have his bedtime milk or story. This may seem painful at the time, but it can help to establish a habit that makes for less stress (and more sleep) for everyone in the long run.

Heighten his bodily awareness

Once your child has learnt to not just 'wee anywhere, anytime', he may need help remembering to use the potty. Some parents find that, after around 18 months, their child has the inclination to simply hold on as long as possible. This can cause problems. If he becomes so used to holding on and ignoring the sensation of a full bladder (or bowel) then he can begin to lose awareness of it. Also, he can actually damage his bladder and bowel by overstretching it. Some children are more prone to this than others. Children who find it hard to tell when they are tired, hungry or cold are more likely to need help recognising that they need to pass waste too. Help him with toileting in the same way that you help for meals, clothing and bedtimes.

If your child is very involved in his play, there may be times when you need to suggest that he uses the potty. Try to provide a learning opportunity. Look for a pause in his play where you can engage him and make a connection. Then draw his attention to the body language that is telling you that he needs to go: 'Why are you doing that with your legs? You seem to be wriggling around a lot. Do you feel more comfortable if you squeeze your willy?' Try to let him work out for himself that he needs a wee. Sometimes, if he doesn't want to interrupt his play, you can say something like: 'Are you doing that so you can keep the wee in?'

Help him understand his bodily functions

Even if your child has used the potty his whole life, he may still not understand what's going on inside his body. Perhaps he thinks that he can hold on to a full bladder indefinitely, and that wee comes out because he wasn't holding tight enough. It's really important to explain how the body works in a way that he can understand. Understanding can help with co-operation. These examples may help:

'What a big wee! That must be because you drank so much milk!'

(Pointing at a poo.) 'Oh look! I can see some of the sweetcorn that you ate yesterday.'

Anatomical pictures of the body may also help, though it's hard to know how much is understood from a 2D drawing. Models can be better at demonstrating. Here's a fun one that we tried: a weeing robot. Construct a robot out of a cardboard box. Put a funnel at its mouth, and attach an empty water bomb balloon on the inside. Keep giving the robot 'drinks' of water with a funnel through its mouth. Every now and then you and your child can help the robot 'wee' by emptying the water bomb. You could also use a jam jar. You can buy 'wetting' dolls that do the same sort of job.

To illustrate the passage of faeces through the body, you could push dried beans or marbles through a long balloon (the kind used for balloon modelling). Get your toddler to help squeeze the marbles from one end to the other. These balloon tricks help to teach that holding can be dangerous. 'Oh no, there are too many beans! Don't let it break!'

Make sure you tread lightly: you need to emphasise the importance of regular potty use, without provoking fear.

Realistic expectations

Abandoning nappies does not mean you should expect your child to be accident free. Obviously, it's not fair to get cross or impatient with him for getting it wrong. You're the one who took off the nappies! (Or even if he made the decision to take the nappies off, he didn't fully understand what that might mean.)

Some onlookers may suggest that if your child is having accidents, then they are not 'ready' for potty training. These parents are coming from the 'spontaneous potty training' school of thought, which implies if you wait long enough children will learn all the skills they need while still wearing their nappies, by themselves, without any input from parents. The BLPT method is a different kind of system that involves the parents and toddlers working together to learn the necessary skills. It wouldn't be a learning process without accidents.

It pretty much goes without saying that you need to be patient and realistic with your expectations. But you also have to be aware of going too far the other way. I sometimes hear parents saying to their children, as they clean a poo off the carpet: 'It's okay, don't worry!' This can be unhelpful too. Frankly, it's *not okay* to poo on the carpet, and we shouldn't be telling our children that it is. There is (hopefully) no reason why he should be worried about it, so you don't need to overcompensate and tell him not to worry. You need to strike a balance.

Too much pressure?

Parents often worry if potty training will put too much pressure on their child. The fact is that potty training is an *inherently neutral* act, just like learning to walk, or how to sit at the table to eat. There is no reason why your child should attach feelings of shame or fear to this process. However, we have to recognise that the process is sometimes loaded with these emotions *for us parents*. We may feel like we are being judged in the way we are setting about the process. Perhaps we *especially* feel under pressure at this stage because we have been pottying our babies from a young age. It's quite possible that BLPT was virtually synonymous with early toilet independence in your mind. (And perhaps you even suggested that was the case to family and friends who watched you.) If so, you may feel like you or your child are falling short of expectations.

These ideas are really unhelpful. The key to success here (and, in fact, in parenting in general) is to *accept the way things are*, and then work with that reality to try to bring about the change you want. This is what I mean by *baby-led*. Another way of thinking about it could be *reality-led*. In this case, it might mean accepting that your toddler still resists potty time and finding creative ways to make it fun. It might mean accepting that your toddler never initiates potty trips and embracing the fact that you'll need to initiate them yourself for a while. It could be any kind of scenario: we each have a different reality we need to embrace. If you can joyfully accept the way your child is at this moment, and stay relaxed about where he is on the journey – without losing sight of the destination – you will be doing a great job indeed!

But perhaps it is not so easy for you to stay relaxed about it. Some people associate slow progress on the potty, and particularly accidents, with feelings of shame – perhaps because of their own childhood experiences. If you recognise this happening with you, it's *really* important that you acknowledge those feelings. If you don't, they are sure to interfere with the way you help your child – either by making you feel negative about his progress, or by leading you to overcompensate and send confusing messages (or both).

A useful comparison is to think back to the example of Mosi in Kenya on page 200. In our culture, we can have an impression that society wants to know exactly *when* potty training happened, and *how long* the process took, to judge and compare accordingly. However, Mosi's family barely even notice that he is potty training, and they aren't counting the months and comparing notes with other families. If he wees unexpectedly on the floor at 26 months, they won't be bitterly dejected and think *Oh no – he's not potty trained after all!*

If you can, it's really helpful to let go of the term 'Potty Trained' or 'Not Potty Trained Yet'. These labels are value judgements, which can make us feel criticised, either for our parenting skills, or on behalf of our child. And if your child himself begins to sense this disappointment or criticism, that can be very damaging indeed. I find it more useful to use the phrase: 'He's out of nappies,' and, if you feel like expanding: 'He's out of nappies, though he still has the odd accident, of course.'

> *'When Rose was independent at 12½ months I was so worried we would have a miss. Then a couple of years down the line, long after my daughter was over the whole thing, I saw all my friends go through traditional Western potty training, and the children were having accidents all over the place, with changes of clothes every outing. I wish I hadn't worried so much.'*
>
> **Beth C, mum to Rose, three and a half years**

Maintenance

Once your toddler has the basic idea that he puts his wee and poo in the potty, you still may have to do some maintenance to keep him on the right track. With a child who doesn't tend to self-initiate trips, this means reminding him when he should go.

Insisting

There are two ways to approach insisting. You can either wait until your child is doing 'the wee dance' or you can set up a predictable routine, for example, on waking, around mealtimes and before bed.

It's easier for your child to relate to these kinds of markers than clock times. If he attends nursery, there will probably be times during the day when it makes sense to have a toilet break.

If you need to insist, it's important to stay really calm about it. I like to remember Sarah Napthali's mantra from her book *Buddhism for Mothers*: *'gentle, patient and persistent'*. When I am insisting with my son, I try to make it fun and playful, and I offer him lots of choices. I also sometimes remind him I won't do anything else until it's done.

Hannah has a very clear way of signalling to her daughter, Lily, that she means business. If she needs to physically intervene for some reason (for example, if Lily is pushing another child), then Hannah gives her warning that she is about to overpower her, by counting to five. She counts in a kind – not cross – way. Sometimes Lily stops before she gets to five, and sometimes Hannah has to step in. She sometimes uses this method to get compliance in other areas too – for example, getting in the car seat.

If she thinks Lily is starting to get worked up about using the potty, she tries to change the dynamic. She warns her that she is about to start counting: 'One … two …' Immediately Lily races to get on the potty. This is not through fear, but a kind of playful excitement. It becomes a game to see if she can get there in time. Hannah doesn't overuse the strategy. Afterwards Lily is relaxed and happy; an upset has been averted. Not every parent will feel comfortable using this method, but for Hannah and Lily it certainly serves to prevent frustration on both sides.

It may seem paradoxical, but children can be more able to accept situations if they feel they don't have any choice about it. (Though you need to make sure you are asking them to do something within their ability *at that moment*.) It's great to give them a free rein where possible. But in areas you feel strongly about, or where you have a superior understanding about safety and health, then sometimes it's best to be utterly firm and non-negotiable. Most children, for example, quickly learn that they mustn't wander into other people's private gardens and pick their flowers. That's because we send them a very clear message about that. We can apply this same firmness to any aspect of behaviour we choose. However, it's important to choose wisely: it takes energy and effort on the part of the parent to stand firm, and if it's done too often, children can feel overwhelmed.

Routines

Some children and families respond really well to routines, and some find them unhelpful. My son always hated going for a wee 'just in case', and rarely performed unless he was bursting, so I avoided routine potty trips with him, with the exception of first thing in the morning and before bed. In contrast, I found that my daughter was more co-operative when we had a regular routine in place. As a toddler she found it hard to transition between activities. This meant that she avoided breaking off her play for the potty, with the result that she would become increasingly uncomfortable and agitated. This impacted her behaviour as it made it even harder for her to self-regulate. The predictability and consistency of a routine helped her become more co-operative and set up clear expectations and boundaries.

It can be hard initially to set a routine in place. Include enjoyable rituals (e.g. saying 'bye-bye wee' as you flush, or ticking a chart) and tack it on to other routine daily events, such as mealtimes or nap time. If you feel it will work for your family, then do persevere. Paradoxically, it can often be the children who most *resist* a routine (or any other kind of instruction) that get the most benefit from it.

The benefits for parents

It's also true that *parents* with somewhat chaotic and irregular days can benefit from a family toilet routine! It can take the stress out of remembering to prompt toilet trips for overstretched parents, becoming 'one less thing to think about'. It can also be particularly useful when someone other than the main carer – partners, grandparents, childminders, etc. – look after your toddler. They may feel more confident with a routine than having to guess or remember to offer toilet trips. (And you may feel more confident that your toddler will get taken to the toilet.) If you have more than one child, it may be that family toilet trips (especially when out and about) are the only way to meet everyone's needs without spending the whole day rushing to and from various toilets.

When I was a young first-time mum, I thought that routine-based parenting was the antithesis of good parenting, and I avoided it at all costs. As my children have grown older, and I've grown a little wiser, I've realised that routines can be a really helpful parenting tool. The important thing is that the routine must *serve the needs of the family*, and never feel like the *family is serving the needs of the routine*.

Letting him take control

Taking an active role in prompting your toddler to use the potty, especially if you stick to a consistent routine, can have a positive effect on your child. It might be that he gets used to the feeling of being comfortable without an overfull bladder, and has an extremely strong association with passing waste and the potty or toilet, so that he completely internalises the process. This can mean that when you reduce the amount of prompting, or even cut it out altogether, he will already have the skills to recognise by himself when he needs to go and will consistently self-initiate potty trips at the appropriate times.

However, it is also quite possible that the opposite is true. It may be that your child becomes (or continues to be) over-reliant on you to initiate his potty trips, without noticing when his bladder is full.

It can be a very practical tool to initiate potty trips to keep your toddler dry – either at a specific time (say on a train journey) or over a period of weeks or months. Long term, however, you want your child to be able to recognise for himself when he needs to go, and for him to take appropriate, timely action. So that your child can do this successfully, he needs to be motivated to keep himself clean and dry – or, at least, he needs to be developmentally ready for that motivation to be cultivated. He also needs to practise. You can't necessarily expect him to get it right straight away. This is when it is useful to stop insisting and let your child take more control.

> Sam was out of nappies for good at around age 20 months. However, his mum, Sarah, needed to prompt him throughout the day, and they followed a regular routine of visiting the toilet before meal and snack times. When Sam was around two and a half, Sarah wanted to help him to take more responsibility for his toileting. She started to hold back from prompting. When he seemed to be very uncomfortable, she tried to suggest the potty in a low-key way. She might move the potty into view, or mention that she herself was going to the loo. Sometimes she asked him why he was wriggling around so much, or whether he was 'all right'.
>
> Sam began to ask for the potty more and more, though often he would wet a little into his pants first. Sarah experimented with not mentioning the potty at all to see what would happen. Although there were a few more incidences of wet pants (not puddles), she noticed that he was asking for the potty more and more reliably. Most days he was completely dry, though sometimes he would still 'leak' a patch of wee before he took himself to the potty. This trend continued over several months, and by the time he was three years old Sarah felt she could leave the house without the need for bringing spare pants.

It can be really hard to make this change as a parent. It takes a certain amount of faith and letting go of control. Perhaps one of the hardest things is accepting that there will almost certainly be *more* accidents. This can be disheartening if your child has been virtually accident free with your help for many months. It can feel like a backwards step. As I mentioned before, parents can feel anxious that others will view their child as 'Not Yet Potty Trained'. Please try to let go of this label! By now your child will fully understand what the potty is for and how to put something in it. He just needs to fine-tune the timing and learn to recognise how long is too long.

A mixed approach

It may well be appropriate for you to switch between the two styles: sometimes insisting or following a routine; sometimes stepping back and letting your toddler initiate. Whether you change styles within a single day, or whether you spend longer periods on each approach, will be for you to judge.

If you do use a routine-based approach or a prompting-based-on-signals approach, then it is certainly worth holding off every now and then, just to see if your child will ask for the potty. He will probably hold on longer than you would like, but he may surprise you by being able to get himself to the potty in good time. It's important to remember that even if he does leave it too long, and leaks a little (or even creates a puddle), he will get better with practice, so it's worth giving him the opportunity.

Bowel mastery

Much of this chapter has focused on bladder control, as this is a much harder skill to master. Because the passing of bowel movements tends to be a much longer process, it is normally easier to guide your toddler towards a potty as soon as he starts grunting or straining. Although my children experimented with pooing in funny places around the one-year mark, when they were gaining voluntary control of the anal sphincter, in general, their transition to 100 per cent reliability was pretty gradual and effortless. This seems to be typical of most children who start potty training before 18 months. However, two main factors can cause problems with bowel training: constipation and entrenched habits.

Constipation

Hard, backed-up faeces can be painful to pass, and children may become frightened of the process and try to hold back, further exacerbating the problem. Your child might then suffer from impaction – when hard faeces remains in the colon and stretches it. Looser matter is then pushed through this hard mass, and into the rectum. However, because of the mixed signals from the bowel, it is very difficult to control this type of soiling. It is extremely important that you seek medical advice if you suspect constipation. Your doctor may recommend laxatives to help clear the bowel and help it to regain its normal size.

Entrenched habits

It is far more likely that entrenched habits will be an issue for children who have been nappied conventionally, but it may also happen where BLPT has been practised part-time. Children begin to make associations about how and where they defecate from the moment they are born – whether that's in a nappy or in a potty. By 18 months, this conditioning can be very strong. If they have been *voluntarily* soiling their nappy for some time, it may be very difficult to persuade them to do otherwise. They can become psychologically attached to using their nappy as a toilet. Parents will gently need to teach them to change their habits; they may require a great deal of support.

Children who have been conditioned to use a potty may experiment with wilfully emptying their bowel into their nappy, but they are likely to find this experience unsettling or uncomfortable. This means that it usually does not take long for them to realign their voluntary inclination (what they decide to do) with their conditioning (what feels right).

Finally there!

True completion is likely to creep up without you realising. Accidents become less and less frequent, and your child takes more and more responsibility for getting to the potty or toilet. You'll probably forget to pack the spare trousers one day, and then realise that it doesn't really matter anyway. The extra niceties, such as bum wiping, hand washing, lowering the lid and flushing, may take a little longer to master, but essentially, you've done it!

Summary

- BLPT completion is different to conventional potty training as the process starts earlier and is more gradual.
- Parents don't have to guess when their child is ready for each stage, and most of the skills necessary for autonomy are in place before they learn consistency.
- Some children transition from BLPT to toilet independence seamlessly, whether through a routine-based approach or a responsive approach.
- Other children, who have used the potty less regularly, or who have gone through periods of resistance, may need extra effort to complete the process.
- Parents can speed up the process by ditching nappies and dedicating time and space to consolidating the learning.

Chapter 16

Night Completion

Night training can be a confusing subject as people mean different things by the process. It can also be extremely daunting, particularly if you have avoided offering the potty in the night before. Children become dry at night in a few different ways, and there is no one right way to set about the process.

Reassessing night-time capabilities

The conventional wisdom is that night-time dryness takes longer to achieve than daytime dryness. The NHS website says that most children learn to stay dry at night between three and five years.[1] In contrast, some families who have been offering the potty from birth report that their children are regularly dry at night from as young as *nine months* – often long before they are out of nappies in the daytime. I don't mention this as a target to aim for, as in many cases night-time dryness at such an age is not within the capabilities of a child. But I think it is useful to bear in mind that our children may be ready for that process *much* earlier than we expect. I think that the main reason for delayed night-time dryness across the general population has far more to do with parents' reluctance to initiate the process than the child's own capabilities.

It's (almost) all about hormones

The first thing we need to understand is that hormones play a very significant part in night-time dryness. In particular, when adults are asleep, the hormone vasopressin acts on the kidneys to instruct them to remove more water from our urine. This means that less urine is produced in the night and it is more concentrated. Thus the first wee in the morning is normally stronger in colour and smell. Babies' bodies do not produce so much vasopressin at first, so the urine they produce in the night may be just as watery as during the day. This means they need to wee at intervals through the night.

As babies grow, they gradually produce more vasopressin, which begins to reduce the amount of urine they produce at night. In many children, this will eventually result in the ability to hold the bladder for up to 12 hours. It is important to note, however, that vasopressin levels vary enormously between people. Many adults need to visit the loo one, or even two, times during an eight-hour sleep. Vasopressin production declines as we head towards old age and it can be suppressed by drinking alcohol. However, it seems that there is very little, if anything, we can do to *boost* its production. In children, the only thing we can do is wait.

When will it kick in?

For some children, you can notice evidence of vasopressin activity from as little as four or five months of age. Both my children occasionally lasted 10 hours through the night without urinating from the age of six months old. This was particularly apparent if the weather was hot. I know of many families whose babies regularly last 10 hours from the age of nine months. My daughter often went this length of time in the night from around 11–12 months. However, it is also possible that the hormone won't really kick in until they are much older – perhaps two or three years, or even older. It may *never* be sufficient for them to last the whole night.

Options if your baby still needs to wee at night

If your child can't last all through the night without urinating, your main options are to do one of the following:

1. Let him wee in the bed while wearing a nappy.
2. Practise BLPT at night and help him to use the potty.

It's completely up to you to work out what is best for your family and child at the time. I normally prioritised sleep. With my children that meant different things: I helped my daughter on the potty at night and my son generally wore a nappy until 24 months. Things can change, however, and while it might seem appropriate to allow a 10-month-old baby to wee in his nappy at night, by the time he is 18, 24 or 30 months, you may have different priorities.

If you have been offering the potty at night

If you have already been offering at night, then it's likely that there will be a relatively seamless transition to night-time dryness. We already know that babies and toddlers tend not to wee when they are asleep. At night they normally rouse themselves or rise into a lighter level of sleep before emptying their bladder. Urinating during deep sleep is uncommon, and can indicate illness or an unusual level of tiredness.

Babies and toddlers who have been using the potty at night may ask for it less and less, until they wee perhaps once a night, then every other night, and then not at all.

It is easy to assist a baby or child who sleeps in the same room as you. If they have moved into their own room, it can seem harder to manage. However, many parents find that they can lift their child for a 'dream wee' (see page 114) at 10 or 11pm. Others find that their child is able to negotiate the potty, or even a visit to the bathroom by themselves. I used to lift my daughter around 10pm when she was

12–18 months. One night she groggily refused the potty. From then on I found that she was normally able to last the night without weeing. When she did need to go, she'd make it pretty clear to me that she needed some help.

If you haven't been offering the potty at night

If you are ready to help your child achieve night-time dryness, but you haven't previously been offering the potty at night, then you will need to change your approach. One of the biggest obstacles to night training is that parents are typically unaware of their child's urination habits. If their child presents them with a wet nappy in the morning (especially a disposable one), it is virtually impossible to tell how often, and when, the urination occurred. This information is vital if you want to take your child out of nappies at night.

There are two ways of finding this out: one is that you can keep checking his nappies to see when they are warm and wet (or take the nappy off altogether and see when the bedding gets wet); or you can make a guess and see if you can catch any wee coming out.

Strategies to aid night completion

Catch the morning wee

In many cases, children continue to wee in their nappy first thing in the morning, long after they are capable of being dry at night, so this is a great place to start. Make a commitment to try to catch this morning wee. Also, you'll need to set this as an expectation for your toddler.

It may be that the nappy itself is making it difficult for your child to get to the potty: he may find it hard to get to and undo his nappy. If your toddler sleeps in a separate room from you, you may need to set your own alarm for a few days, so that you can be present as soon as he wakes up to help him on to the potty or loo. Alternatively, you could try leaving his nappy and pyjama bottoms off, to make it really easy for him (or you).

Holding it

Even if you are successfully catching his morning wee, it may be that your toddler is still regularly weeing at some point during the night. It may be that this is simply a habit. It's quite possible that your toddler knows he is wearing a nappy (perhaps he is out of nappies in the day), and he is used to weeing where he lies. It's pretty convenient. Has he ever been given a different message? It's worth mentioning to him that he can try to 'hold on till morning' – perhaps after he's done his last wee at bedtime. You'll need to approach this with a light touch, as he may not be capable of holding on till morning yet.

I didn't explicitly say this to my son, but when he was 24 months, I took him out of daytime nappies for good and I switched to cloth nappies at night (I had vowed to myself never to use another disposable). The combination of the focus on the potty during the daytime, and the different feel of the nappies at night, meant that my son automatically felt different about weeing in his night nappy. The conditioning to wee in a nappy at night is very strong.

Waiting for the hormones

Many conventional potty-training guides seem to suggest that the only way of achieving night-time dryness is to wait for the vasopressin to kick in and for the child to lose the need to urinate at night at all. They argue that it is perfectly fine for three, four and even five year olds to wear (and wee in) nappies at night. In fact night nappies up to *age 15* are on sale in supermarkets.

As I hope I have made clear, vasopressin is only *one* of the factors that contributes to night-time dryness.

The physical factors, which we *can't* change, are:

- The increase of vasopressin, which reduces the need to urinate
- The bladder capacity increasing, also reducing the need to urinate

The behavioural factors, which we *can* change, are:

- A toddler being motivated to hold his bladder while in bed
- A toddler being motivated to take himself to the potty in the night and in the morning
- The parents helping with, or encouraging, potty use in the night and first thing in the morning

The physical factors massively help in achieving night-time dryness, but it is possible to achieve it even if your child doesn't have the capacity to last all night. In fact, in both the short and the long term, it is extremely desirable for your toddler to know how to keep himself dry if he does happen to need a wee in the night. Occasionally he may drink far more than usual in the evening, or something might stop him settling into a deep sleep so his urine production is higher than normal.

> *'Night completion just happened for all four of my children because we've always used a potty at night. With my third child we still had wet beds occasionally until she was nearly three – sometimes she would get up and most nights I'd lift her for a pre-empt, but on the odd occasion she wet the bed. She started to wake herself and go from around two and a half years. Before then we'd have to notice her awake and sitting in bed, a bit lost, and rescue her!'*
> **Jenn, mum to Connie (seven years), Jamie (five years), Abbey (three years) and Rosie (nineteen months)**

Occasional accidents

Wet beds may still occur, even after night-time dryness has been achieved. Once my daughter was out of night nappies (at 15 months), and for the next two years, she would sometimes need to use the toilet in the night, sometimes she would sleep through without weeing and occasionally she would wet the bed. Bed-wetting usually occurred in

The effect of milk at night

Parents often wonder about the connection between drinking and weeing at night. I've already spoken about this in Chapter 7, though it is useful to revisit the subject when your toddler is older than 18 months. Many parents are concerned that their toddler's habit of a big bedtime drink makes them need to wee in the night. They may also have breast milk, a bottle or water in the night. Sometimes childcare experts dismiss breastfeeding at night, suggesting that it is only 'for comfort', and that their milk intake is minimal. In fact, toddlers can take in significant quantities of milk in the night when they are one, two or even three years old. Common sense tells us that there must be a link between intake of fluids and urine production.

However, this connection is not as direct as one might think. As mentioned earlier, toddlers' production levels of vasopressin go up as they grow, as does their bladder capacity. This means that, even if they drink half a pint of milk or more in the night, their body works slowly to process it; the kidneys take out much of the water, and their bladder may be big enough to store the remainder right through until morning. I found that, even though my two-year-old son was drinking lots of milk at bedtime *and during the night*, he was still able to last the entire night without weeing.

Having said that, we would be unwise to let our children go to sleep on a full bladder, or give them pints of milk at bedtime. In our family, we always insisted on a bedtime wee, either just before lying down, or right before breastfeeding to sleep.

spates, with two or three episodes during a week. It was a nightmare for my washing! These episodes were almost invariably followed by a heavy cold or other illness. It was striking that bed-wetting normally happened when she was in a deep sleep. This meant that no amount of 'training' would have been able to prevent them. They stopped happening after the age of about three and a half.

We parents sometimes have a tendency to panic whenever 'regression' occurs, and think that we need to act fast to get things back on track. In the case of bed-wetting – especially if it comes after a period of being dry at night – I think that it is best to wait for a week or two to see if the situation resolves itself. It may well be caused by illness, or by some other disturbance such as a holiday or new baby.

Summary

- As babies grow, physical changes mean they are less likely to need to wee at night:
  o The hormone vasopressin reduces the volume of urine produced
  o Their bladder capacity increases
- Parents can also teach their toddler behaviours that keep him dry at night:
  o Encourage him to 'hold on'
  o Lift him for a 'dream wee' at night
  o Encourage or help him use the potty during the night
  o Set an expectation that he should use the potty first thing in the morning
- Occasional wet beds are normal, and may indicate illness or other disruption.

Final Thoughts

'It is so rewarding. Every catch always amazed me that WE did that – they would let me know in their subtle way and I had a strong feeling of being very proud of the both of us. A lot of things about parenting, especially the first time around, can be such a muddle, but BLPT just always made sense!'

**Shyann, mum to Duncan, nine years,
and Hamish, four and a half years**

Offering the potty from birth or in the early months is not for everyone. Some parents will find that the conventional nappy route works better for them. However, I think that it is essential that parents have the information, the resources and the support they need to make *an informed choice.*

In our current mode of thinking, the potty-training period is seen as a time of inconvenience, chaos and anxiety. Often parents have strict time limits – a week off work, or before he starts preschool, or by the time the new baby arrives. Health authorities and childcare experts argue that the later potty training is initiated, the shorter the period of training. In some cases, however, parents may find that they have missed 'the window of opportunity' for their child, and toilet training becomes a protracted and difficult affair.

The received notion is that the *shorter* the potty-training period, the *better*. This view is founded on the assumption that a day, week or month of potty training is *worse* than a day, week or month of full-time nappies. But there are plenty of reasons why wearing nappies isn't desirable: cost, landfill, nappy rash, hygiene, handling faeces – to name a few. Otherwise, why would we bother toilet training at all? Why do we have a perception that potty training is worse than all that?

I think the stress associated with conventional potty training is often *due* to the fact that we start from scratch and try to cram it into as few days as possible. And there's the added stress of choosing when to begin and the pressure to succeed. However, when you embrace the process of learning to use the potty, and work with your baby to allow him to acquire and practise the many skills needed, at his own pace, the whole process can become a joyful experience. And you can find real, tangible, gains – every day. You don't have to wait until potty training is completed. In fact, from the very first catch, you see a direct reduction in the negative qualities of nappies: there will be less cost, less waste, less nappy rash, better hygiene, less faeces to handle … and so on.

Parents understand that the transition from sucking milk to good table manners takes years to perfect, and we delight in the process: videoing our babies as they smear soup over their faces, clothes and floor; joyfully noting the first time they manage to spear a carrot on a fork, or cut a sausage with a knife. BLPT from birth embraces the journey in the same way. We can celebrate when our child responds to a cue, reaches out for a potty, pulls down his own pants or says 'wee-wee' for the first time. We know mess is sometimes part of the process: we just clean it up.

But what about the inconvenience – having to keep half an eye on your baby all the time? This is perhaps what people see as the main drawback to the baby-led approach to potty training. Parents may worry they will have to be on constant alert. And, yes, potty training (at any age) *does* require parents to spend time being alert to their baby's needs. But what parent *doesn't* do this in the first few weeks? And this 'extra' attention has such remarkable pay-offs. It doesn't just offer practical benefits; parents find that it opens a whole new channel of communication and interaction with their babies. *We are getting to know our babies better.* And that means communicating more often, gaining in confidence and strengthening the parent–baby bond.

In fact, many parents who help their baby pass waste don't even consider themselves to be potty training. For them, the benefits of offering the potty are entirely self-evident, in the moment. *They enjoy the process for its own sake.* They know how to help their baby pass a difficult stool; they can soothe and settle their baby at night; they enjoy his delight as he wees on the bushes. They love the confidence it gives them in handling their baby and communicating with him. They enjoy saving nappies. They enjoy knowing why he may be unsettled. This experience teaches us that potty training doesn't have to be 'a necessary evil' – to be crammed into as short a time as possible.

I hope this book has helped you to delight in the process of BLPT as much as I have done – whether you just use the technique occasionally, or as a full-time alternative to nappies and conventional potty training. You may find the BLPT journey provides some of the tenderest memories of your child's babyhood, and helps create a deeper bond that lasts long beyond the end of potty training.

Glossary

baby-led potty training (BLPT) – a method of assisting your baby to pass waste and helping him learn how to use a potty from birth.

catches – these happen when you successfully predict when your baby needs to pass waste and help him go in the desired place (e.g. when wee lands in the potty).

completion – the phase of BLPT that leads to complete toilet independence.

cues – the sounds, words and gestures you use to communicate to your baby that it is the right time to go (e.g. a 'pssss' sound).

dream wee – lifting a sleeping baby in the night and helping him on the potty.

elimination communication (or EC) – the American name for BLPT.

false potty – when you mistakenly think that a baby needs to go.

misses – these happen when baby wees or poos in his nappy (or the floor/play-mat/other undesirable place) when you were hoping to catch the waste.

potty pause – a period of time when lots of misses occur, sometimes combined with resistance to the potty.

signals – the unique behaviours a baby displays that indicate he needs to pass waste. These may be conscious or unconscious.

to hold a baby out – to hold a baby in a position where he can defecate and urinate outside his nappy.

to potty – a verb meaning to help a baby pass waste by helping him into the optimum position, e.g. *I pottied him as soon as he woke up.*

References

Chapter 1: What is Baby-Led Potty Training?

1) The Disposable Diaper Industry Source, 'Diapers Need in the Next 20 Years', http://disposablediaper.net/general-information/diapers-need-in-the-next-20-years [accessed 8 January 2015].

2) London Borough of Hounslow, 'Real Nappy Scheme', http://www.hounslow.gov.uk/reusable_nappies [accessed 8 January 2015].

3) BBC Climate, 'Methane', http://www.bbc.co.uk/climate/evidence/methane.shtml [accessed 8 January 2015].

4) Jansson, U.B., Hanson, M., Hanson, E., Hellström, A.L. and Sillén, U., 'Voiding pattern in healthy children 0 to 3 years old: a longitudinal study', *The Journal of Urology*, 164(6) (2000), pp. 2,050–4.

5) Duong, T.H., Jansson, U.B., Holmdahl, G., Sillén, U. and Hellström, A.L., 'Development of bladder control in the first year of life in children who are potty trained early', *Journal of Pediatric Urology*, 6(5) (2010), pp. 501–5.

6) deVries, M.W. and deVries, M.R., 'Cultural relativity of toilet training readiness: a perspective from East Africa', *Pediatrics*, 60(2) (1977), pp. 170–7.

7) Klein, Josephine, *Samples from English Cultures, Volume 2* (London: Routledge and Kegan Paul, 1965), pp. 449–52.

8) Brazelton, T. Berry, 'A Child-Oriented Approach to Toilet Training', *Pediatrics*, 29 (1962), pp. 121–8.

9) The Disposable Diaper Industry Source, 'Diapers Need in the Next 20 Years', http://disposablediaper.net/general-information/diapers-need-in-the-next-20-years [accessed 8 January 2015].

10) Margulis, Jennifer, *The Business of Baby: What Doctors Don't Tell You, What Corporations Try to Sell You, and How to Put Your Pregnancy, Childbirth, and Baby Before Their Bottom Line* (Simon and Schuster, 2013), p. 173.

11) Sonna, Linda, *Early-Start Potty Training* (McGraw-Hill, 2005), pp. 5–6.

12) Goode, Erica, 'Two Experts Do Battle Over Potty Training', *The New York Times* (12 January 1999), http://www.nytimes.com/1999/01/12/us/two-experts-do-battle-over-potty-training.html [accessed 3 December 2014].

13) BabyCenter, 'When did you start and finish potty training your child?', http://www.babycenter.com/viewPollResults.htm?pollId=1478320 [accessed 8 January 2015].

14) NHS Choices, 'Potty problems and toilet training tips' (2014), http://www.nhs.uk/conditions/pregnancy-and-baby/pages/potty-training-tips.aspx#close [accessed 22 August 2014].

15) Ibid.

Chapter 2: The Biology of Toilet Training

1) Jansson, U.B., Hanson, M., Hanson, E., Hellström, A.L. and Sillén, U., 'Voiding pattern in healthy children 0 to 3 years old: a longitudinal study', *The Journal of Urology*, 164 (6) (2000), pp. 2,050–4.

2) Brazelton, T. Berry, 'A Child-Oriented Approach to Toilet Training', *Pediatrics*, 29 (1962), pp. 121–8.

3) This phenomenon was demonstrated by the recent study following Vietnamese infants from birth to 24 months: Duong, T.H., Jansson, U.B. and Hellström, A.L., 'Vietnamese mothers' experiences with potty training procedure for children from birth to 2 years of age', *Journal of Pediatric Urology*, 9 (2013), pp. 808–14.

4) Duong, T.H., Jansson, U.B., Holmdahl, G., Sillén, U. and Hellström, A.L., 'Development of bladder control in the first year of life in children who are potty trained early', *Journal of Pediatric Urology*, 6(5) (2010), pp. 501–5.

5) Fowler, C.J., Griffiths, D. and de Groat, W.C., 'The neural control of micturition', *Nature Reviews Neuroscience*, 9 (2008), p. 453.

6) deVries, M.W. and deVries, M.R., 'Cultural relativity of toilet training readiness: a perspective from East Africa', *Pediatrics*, 60(2) (1977), pp. 170–7.

7) Blum, N.J., Taubman, B. and Nemeth, N., 'Relationship between age at initiation of toilet training and duration of training: a prospective study', *Pediatrics*, 111(4) (2003), pp. 810–14.

Chapter 4: Getting Started

1) Babiesfirstlactation, 'The Newborn's Stomach', http://babies firstlactation.wordpress.com/2013/08/09/the-newborns-stomach/ [accessed 11 August 2014].

Chapter 5: Nappies and Clothing

1) Rose, Clare, *Children's Clothes: Since 1750* (London: Batsford, 1989).

Chapter 7: BLPT at Night

1) Born Ready: Baby-led Potty Training, 'Pre-emptive evening wee (17 months)' (2013), https://www.youtube.com/watch?v= Bw1Xn9AMG_0 [accessed 13 August 2014].

2) Tracy Hogg and Melinda Blau, *Secrets of the Baby Whisperer: How to Calm, Connect and Communicate with your Baby*, (London: Vermilion, 2001).

Chapter 8: Special Cases

1) PromoCon, 'Information Sheet on Toilet Training Children with Special Needs' (2011).

Chapter 10: Developmental Changes at 6-12 Months

1) Hodges, Steve, 'A Doctor Responds: Don't Potty Train Your Baby', *Huffington Post* (2012), http://www.huffingtonpost.com/steve-hodges-md/potty-training_b_1424826.html [accessed 8 August 2014].

2) Blum, N.J., Taubman, B., Nemeth, N., 'Relationship between age at initiation of toilet training and duration of training: a prospective study', *Pediatrics*, 111(4) (2003), pp. 810–14.

3) Russo, Marina and others, 'Stool Consistency, but Not Frequency, Correlates with Total Gastrointestinal Transit Time in Children', *The Journal of Pediatrics*, 162(6) (2013), pp. 1,188–92, doi: http://dx.doi.org/10.1016/j.jpeds.2012.11.082.

4) Garcia, Joseph, *Sign with Your Baby: How to Communicate with Infants Before They Can Speak*, (Seattle, Washington: Northlight Communications, 2002).

Chapter 13: Moving Towards Toilet Independence (12-18 months)

1) Brazelton, T. Berry, 'A Child-Oriented Approach to Toilet Training', *Pediatrics*, 29 (1962), pp. 121–8.

2) Newson, John and Elizabeth, *Patterns of Infant Care in an Urban Community* (London: George Allen and Unwin, 1963), p. 122.

3) Ibid., p. 123.

4) Duong, T.H., Jansson U.B. and Hellström, A.L., 'Vietnamese mothers' experiences with potty training procedure for children from birth to 2 years of age', *Journal of Pediatric Urology*, 9 (2013), pp. 808–14.

Chapter 15: Day Completion

1) NHS Choices, 'Potty problems and toilet training tips' (2014), http://www.nhs.uk/conditions/pregnancy-and-baby/pages/potty-training-tips.aspx#close [accessed 22 August 2014].

2) Adapted from: deVries, M.W. and deVries, M.R., 'Cultural relativity of toilet training readiness: a perspective from East Africa', *Pediatrics*, 60(2) (1977), pp. 170–77.

Chapter 16: Night Completion

1) NHS Choices, 'Potty problems and toilet training tips' (2014), http://www.nhs.uk/conditions/pregnancy-and-baby/pages/potty-training-tips.aspx#close [accessed 22 August 2014].

Resources

Books

BLPT/elimination communication

Bauer, Ingrid, *Diaper Free: The Gentle Wisdom of Natural Infant Hygiene* (New York: Plume, 2006)

Boucke, Laurie, *Infant Potty Training: A Gentle and Primeval Method Adapted to Modern Living*, second edition (Lafayette, Colorado: Colin White & Laurie Boucke, 2002)

Gross-Loh, Christine, *The Diaper-Free Baby: The Natural Toilet Training Alternative* (New York: William Morrow Paperbacks, 2007)

Sonna, Linda, *Early-Start Potty Training* (New York: McGraw-Hill Contemporary, 2005)

Other parenting books

Cohen, Lawrence J., *Playful Parenting*, reprint edition (New York: Ballantine Books, 2012)

Garcia, Joseph, *Sign with Your Baby: How to Communicate with Infants Before They Can Speak* (Seattle, Washington: Northlight Communications, 2002)

Jackson, Deborah, *Baby Wisdom: The World's Best-Kept Secrets for the First Year of Parenting* (London: Hodder and Stoughton, 2002)

Napthali, Sarah, *Buddhism for Mothers: A Calm Approach to Caring for Yourself and Your Children* (Crows Nest, NSW: Allen & Unwin, 2011)

Websites

BLPT/elimination communication information

www.nappyfreebaby.co.uk

A site that provides information on BLPT basics and suppliers of BLPT-related equipment, a consultation service, workshops, a nursery factsheet and a forum.

www.bornready.uk

A site providing information on BLPT and related workshops, plus a forum. Also the home of Flaparaps – the drop-flap nappy.

General information and support

www.nct.org.uk

This charity offers a wide range of information, social activities and events to help support parents.

www.babywearing.co.uk/sling-meet/

A site offering information on 'Sling Meets': regular events that help parents learn more about babywearing and meet other like-minded parents.

www.singandsign.com

Sing and Sign offer information on baby signing and how to find singing classes near you.

www.laleche.org.uk

A breastfeeding support organisation which runs local support groups.

www.thebabycafe.org

Baby Café runs a network of breastfeeding support drop-in centres.

Special needs

www.mommajorje.com
A parenting blog following the story of BLPT with a child with Down's syndrome.

www.disabledliving.co.uk/PromoCon/
PromoCon promotes awareness and support for continence issues in people with disabilities.

Acknowledgements

Thank you to Jane of Graham Maw Christie, who saw the potential in this book and has been so supportive ever since. Thanks to Sam Jackson at Vermilion, who expertly helped shape up the manuscript and has patiently guided me through the publication process. Especial thanks to my copyeditor, Louise Francis, who prodded and poked with such thoroughness and good humour. Thanks to Mum, and to Dad. Thanks to Isabel Gregory, who lent me her house to write in. Becky Hatch, Jen Cottril, Ben Brettell, Sarah Travis and Rachel Derrick all provided invaluable commentary – thank you! Jenn Conn of bornready.uk deserves a special mention for her good friendship, and the generosity and energy with which she promotes BLPT. I couldn't have done it without my dear friend Antonia King, who sewed me my first pair of rainbow chaps, and who stayed up till 1am commenting on my final draft. Ruth Collins provided unconditional support throughout the writing of this book – thank you.

And of course, thanks to my wonderful husband, Alex Ogg, who has pottied our children as enthusiastically as I have (and drew the beautiful pictures in these pages). And the biggest thanks of all goes to our children, which is where it all began.

Index

Index